iu Title Source 3 - 10/11

Ancient Peoples and Places

THE
MYCENAEANS

General Editor

DR. GLYN DANIEL

Ancient Peoples and Places

THE
MYCENAEANS

Lord William Taylour

66 PHOTOGRAPHS
67 LINE DRAWINGS
4 MAPS
3 TABLES

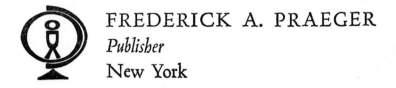

FREDERICK A. PRAEGER
Publisher
New York

THIS IS VOLUME THIRTY-NINE IN THE SERIES

Ancient Peoples and Places

GENERAL EDITOR: DR. GLYN DANIEL

BOOKS THAT MATTER

Published in the United States of America in 1964
by Frederick A. Praeger, Inc., Publisher
64 University Place, New York 3, N.Y.
All rights reserved
© Lord William Taylour 1964
First Published 1964
Library of Congress Catalog Card Number : 64–17680
Printed in Holland

CONTENTS

ILLUSTRATIONS

Preface

THE TASK OF PRODUCING this book proved greater than I had expected and was subject to frequent interruptions, of which the most insistent was my annual commitment to excavate in Greece each summer, and all the preparations and aftermath that these undertakings entail. But what I have found most daunting is the task of compressing into forty thousand words the story of one of the great civilizations of history, on which many erudite tomes have appeared, not to mention works on such special aspects as art, religion, or the epics. More recently a rich literature has been occasioned by the decipherment of the Mycenaean script known as Linear B. Tsountas and Manatt, writing in the late nineteenth century and at the dawn of Mycenaean archaeology produced an admirable work called *The Mycenaean Age* which ran to some 110,000 words. It described itself as 'A Study of the Monuments and Cultures of preHomeric Greece'. Much of what is written there is still valid, but much is now perforce outofdate. The present work covers the same kind of material but cannot for a moment claim to be as comprehensive. With the vast increase in later discoveries this book has to be selective and the selection called for may not always meet with general approval.

A latecomer in the field, I have been fortunate in serving my apprenticeship in excavations under two of the most distinguished of Mycenaean archaeologists, Professor Wace and Professor Blegen. I owe them an incalculable debt. To the great loss of archaeology, Professor Wace died in 1957 and I have been deprived of his expert advice in writing this book; Professor Blegen has generously assisted me in countless ways. He has allowed me to use the material and photographs from his excavations in which I had the honour to take part, and he has afforded me valuable counsel and criticism on those parts of the text that have been submitted to him. But my grateful thanks are not only due to him but to those who have spared of their time to read and comment on those aspects of the book on which they are acknowledged experts: Dr J. Chadwick, Mr Vincent R. d'A. Desborough, Mrs E. B. French, Professor W. K. C. Guthrie, the Reverend V. E. G. Kenna, Dr F. H. Stubbings, and Mr Charles K. Williams. I am particularly in-debted to Dr Chadwick and Dr Stubbings. The former read much of the text, the latter all of it. I also wish to thank my friend, Mr B. H. I. H. Stewart, for his many practical and informed suggestions. I have not succeeded in doing justice to all the opinions and criticisms offered to me and in some cases I have gone against them. Particularly has this been the case where the evidence allows of more than one interpretation; obviously in a book of this circumscribed nature it has not been possible to discuss differing theories adequately.

Acknowledgment of permission to use plates and text-figures has been made elsewhere in this book, but I should especially like to thank Mrs Helen Wace for her kindness in allowing me to reproduce plates and figures from her excellent *Mycenae Guide*. Others who have placed me in their debt by the considerable trouble they have taken to obtain the necessary illustrative mat-erial for me are Professor C. W. Blegen, Professor J. L. Caskey, Miss Alison Frantz, Professor Jessen, Mr Robert McCabe, Miss Marion Rawson, Mr E. Stikas, Dr F. H. Stubbings, Thames & Hudson, and Dr N. Verdelis. Many of the text-figures have had to be specially drawn. This work, with the exception of one drawing by Mr M. Spink, has been carried out by Mr M. L. Rowe. Two maps have been drawn by Mr H.A. Shelley. To them I wish to express my best thanks for their excellent work and, not least, to Mrs Ruth Daniel who went to so much trouble in organizing these tasks for me. Through the generosity of Señor F. Collantes de Teran I have been allowed to include information from his interesting excavation of the Dolmen of Matarrubilla, near Seville. I am most grateful to him for his co-operation. I am indebted to Mr D. A. Theochares for information about the Karditsa tholos tomb. Finally, I should like to thank Dr Glyn Daniel and the publishers for the encouragement they have given me and for the patience they have exercised in waiting so long for the writing of this book.

W.D.T.

Introduction

THE MYCENAEANS is not a designation that will be found in the Classical authors. To the Greeks their earliest an-cestors were known under several names. Homer refers to them variously as Achaeans, as Danaans, and as Argives. What the Greeks themselves knew about their early history had come down to them in the form of epic and of numerous legends that were often contradictory. And legendary their remote past re-mained as late as the middle of the nineteenth century. One of the centres of these legends was Mycenae, the ancient capital of Greece and city of Agamemnon, the most powerful of the Greek kings in the Homeric epic of the *Iliad* and leader of the Achaean hosts against Troy. In 1876 legend became history.

Heinrich Schliemann, a retired German merchant, who had amassed a great fortune, decided to employ his wealth in pro-ving a long-cherished theory, namely, that the *Iliad* was not pure fiction, as was often maintained by the Classical pundits of his day, but was historic fact. If Mycenae was indeed Agamem-non's city, some material remains must have survived to de-monstrate it. And so began that series of excavations at Myce-nae, which others on and off have continued to the present day. The first campaign produced sensational results, the unearth-ing of royal burials accompanied by a wealth of funerary equipment in gold, silver, bronze, ivory, pottery, with gold predominating. Schliemann very naturally recognised in these burials the mortal remains of Agamemnon and his followers but in this he was mistaken. He could not know at that time that he had uncovered the tombs of a royal dynasty that reigned some 300 years before the Trojan War.

His mistake is understandable for he was relying on an ac-count given by Pausanias, an indefatigable Baedeker of the

15

second century AD. Pausanias visited Mycenae and was shown the alleged tombs of Agamemnon and of those who were massacred with him. These were said to have been buried within the citadel walls while Clytemnestra and her paramour, Aegisthus (see p. 173), were without the walls, for they were not considered worthy to be buried within the citadel. And to this day the story is perpetuated in the names given to two great vaulted monuments near the citadel, the one datable to the fifteenth century and known as the 'Tomb of Aegisthus', and the other to the thirteenth century and called the 'Tomb of Clytemnestra'. The tombs obviously have no connection with the legend or the local tradition.

But if Schliemann's identifications were at fault, he rightly claimed that he had discovered a new world for archaeology. Through his enterprise a forgotten civilization was reborn and took its name from the city that contained, and now revealed to posterity, the manifold secrets of its history, the epitome of an era that came to be known as the Mycenaean Age. Later research and excavation showed that this civilization pervaded not only the Greek mainland but the Aegean islands and countries bordering on the central and eastern Mediterranean. Sir Flinders Petrie in his excavations at Tell el-Amarna in Egypt had already unearthed a non-Egyptian style of pottery, which with prophetic insight he had labelled 'Aegean'. With Schliemann's discoveries it could now be placed in its proper context. But though Mycenae might be the most important city in Greece at this time, it must not be supposed that there were not other centres of consequence on the mainland and elsewhere that shared the same culture but were nevertheless largely independent. This was to become apparent as later work in the field progressed.

Schliemann's campaigns at Mycenae were largely confined to the Grave Circle, source of the fabulous treasures referred to above. At nearby Tiryns he uncovered, with the able assistance

Fig. 26
Fig. 32

of the architect, Dr Dörpfeld, the foundations of a Mycenaean palace. He also dug at Orchomenos and in Ithaca. All these place-names occur in the *Iliad*, and, as the last-named was the home of Odysseus, much was expected from it, but the results were disappointing. After Schliemann, the Greek Archaeological Society continued excavations at Mycenae. Tsountas, a most distinguished and gifted archaeologist, uncovered the bare remains of a ruined palace on the peak of the acropolis that at one time had housed the royal state of Agamemnon. He excavated houses within the walls of the citadel and the graves of the mighty outside it, including some of the nine tholoi, or vaulted tombs of kings, that have so far been discovered at Mycenae, and the chamber tombs of their wealthier subjects, the majority having been robbed in antiquity.

Fig. 19

In the 1920's the British School at Athens under the inspired direction of Professor A. J. B. Wace carried out many fruitful campaigns both within and without the citadel. His scientific approach enabled him to cast new light on old problems; the results of his work, particularly in connection with the chamber tombs that he dug, contributed to the creation of a sound Mycenaean chronology. In evolving this time-sequence he collaborated with Professor Carl W. Blegen, another great Mycenaean archaeologist. Other contributions by Professor Wace in later years were the discovery of the Prehistoric Cemetery outside the walls (of which Schliemann's Grave Circle was at one time a part), and a number of houses in the lower town, several of which yielded magnificent ivories, finely carved stone vases, and clay tablets inscribed in Linear B (see Chapter I). But one of the most thrilling events of recent times was the finding of a second Grave Circle, this time outside the citadel, which came near to rivalling in the wealth of its grave furniture Schliemann's original discovery. Grave Circle B, as it is called, was excavated by the Greek Archaeological Society under the direction of the late Dr John Papademetriou with

Fig. 36

Fig. 27

Fig. 1. Greece and the Aegean

Thrace

Troad

Phrygia

Troy

Lydia

Anatolia

Chios

Samos

Miletus

elos

Cos

Knidos

Triandha

Rhodes

Dodecanese

C. Gelidonya

ios
ılia
ssos
t
e

H.A.S.

great precision and care, which helped towards the solution of certain problems raised by Schliemann's excavation.

The archaeological schools of many countries have helped towards elucidating the many and varied aspects of the Mycenaean Age (*c.* 1550–1100 BC). Sometimes this was the main object of an excavation, at other times it was the by-product of a campaign primarily concerned with earlier or later periods, as for instance in the American excavations of the Athenian agora. Most of the work of the foreign schools has been concentrated in the Peloponnese, the home of so many of the heroic legends. Apart from Mycenae the British School has excavated in Laconia, Ithaca, and Northern Greece (Macedonia and Thessaly). The Americans have been active in Corinthia, the Argolid, and, most important of all, in Messenia where Professor

Fig. 33

Blegen has uncoverd the best-preserved of the Mycenaean palaces, the palace of the Homeric hero, sage Nestor, King of Pylos. The French School, long established in Greece, is principally known for its magnificent campaigns at Delphi and Delos, devoted to the later historic period, but at these places Mycenaean remains have also been found. Purely Mycenaean

Fig. 41

have been its excavations of a palace at Gla in Boeotia and chamber tombs near Argos. The Germans conducted many campaigns at Tiryns and smaller excavations in other parts of Greece: Attica, Aegina, Salamis, western Messenia, Orchomenos, and north Thessaly. Important work has been carried out by the Swedish School in Messenia, but particularly in the Argolid: Asine, Midea (Dendra), Berbati. The Greek Archaeological Service has naturally played the dominant role in the archaeological field. Its activities need no enumeration as they cover the whole of Greece and the islands.

The Italians have made valuable contributions to the archaeology of the Greek islands and in their own country have uncovered Mycenaean pottery in Sicily and south Italy, in many of the regions in fact that were to form what later came to be known as Magna Graecia in the great colonization period of the eighth-sixth centuries BC. In Greek territory they have excavated in Lemnos, Crete, and Rhodes. Rhodes was an important Mycenaean centre but up till now most of the finds from there have been from tombs. Only one settlement, Triand-ha, has been dug. The British had actually discovered several tombs on the island before the Italians were established there, in fact before Schliemann started excavating at Mycenae, but at that time the true significance of the pottery was not realised. A similar situation existed in Cyprus in the middle of the nine-teenth century. That island is honeycombed with tombs and Mycenaean vases were often found in them, though local wares formed the greater part of the grave furniture. In recent years our knowledge of Mycenaean Cyprus has been considerably increased by excellent work carried out by several nationalities: Cypriot, French, Swedish, British, and American. Important towns and settlements are being, or have been, uncovered: Enkomi (Cypriot and French), Kition (Cypriot), and Vouni (Swedish). Among the other Greek islands that have been ex-plored by foreign schools particular mention should be made of Melos where the British carried out an important excavation in the early part of this century at the site of Phylakopi. Recent archaeological work has been done on Chios (British), Samos (German), and Keos (American).

The origins of Mycenaean civilization exercised archaeolog-ical minds at an early stage and interest naturally turned to-wards Crete which, according to Greek legend and tradition, had had long and intimate relations with the mainland in the heroic age. Schliemann himself had hoped to dig at Knossos but this role fell to Sir Arthur Evans who in 1900 started his epoch-making campaigns there, which established Crete as one of the great powers of the Bronze Age in the Aegean. He was so struck by the markedly Cretan character of Mycenaean art in its early stages that he was led to believe that Greece, or at least the southern part of it, was at one time a Cretan colony. This theory, for long popular, has few adherents today. Evans's extensive and famous campaigns at Knossos have naturally tended to overshadow the work done by other foreign nationalities on the island, but the excavations of the Americans, French, and particularly the Italians have often produced results of equal value and importance.

A natural question that arose from all this archaeological activity was the identity and origin of the people who created the Mycenaean civilization. It was grudgingly admitted that they were the ancestors of the Greeks, but how Greek were they? What is certain is that during its whole history Greece has been subject to the influx of foreign peoples, more often coming with hostile intent. In Classical times the population was already mixed but, whatever the admixture throughout the course of centuries, the resulting culture has been purely Greek. Can one say that the Mycenaean Age marks the beginning of the 'Greek Miracle'? In a sense, yes. Archaeologically it can be demonstrated that there is a cultural continuity right through to the Classical period, but this unbroken continuity stretches backward in time also. There is no recognizable break until about 1900 or 1800 BC, the approximate dating of the change from Early to Middle Bronze Age in Greece. At that time a new and very distinctive type of pottery known as Grey Minyan Ware starts to appear all over Greece. (It was so called by Schliemann who first came across it in his excavations at Orchomenos. He named it after the Minyan tribe who according to legend were associated with that city. This was unfortunate as they in no way could be claimed as the originators of this pottery.) This pottery is easily recognizable from all other grey wares by its superior quality and very special technique, a technique that the invaders, who seem to have been a nomadic tribe, brought with them. The forms of the vases imitate metal ware and their texture suggests that they are copies of silver

Fig. 2

Fig. 2. Middle Helladic pottery. a. matt painted jug from Mycenae; b.c. Minyan ware from Korakou. (after Wace and Stubbings)

vessels. Now this same Grey Minyan Ware is also found in con-siderable abundance throughout the Troad (north-west Tur-key) and is the distinctive pottery of Troy VI; it is indeed one of the criteria that signalises the arrival of a usurping power in that city and the foundation of the Sixth Settlement in the nine-teenth century approximately. The almost simultaneous ap-pearance of this pottery in two separate but not far distant areas suggests that the invaders of the Troad and Greece are one and the same people and it is generally believed that they introduced a form of the Greek tongue into Greece at this time.

The linguistic evidence does not contradict the archaeologi-cal findings and indirectly supports them. It has long been re-cognised that certain place-names ending in -nthos, -ssos, and -ttos such as Zakynthos, Parnassos, Hymettos are non-Greek, or rather pre-Greek. Such names are not only found in Greece but throughout the Aegean (including Crete and west Turkey), an area that was to a large extent culturally homogeneous during the Early Bronze Age. However, from the philological standpoint, the problem of the origin of the Greek language has to be tackled from the other end of the time scale, viz., from the data existing in the eighth century BC when the Greek alphabet first came into use. At that time there were four main groups of dialects of the Greek language: Aeolic, Ionic, Doric, and Arcado-Cypriot. The break-up into dialects from the mother tongue seems to have occurred, according to recent research, in Greece itself. A very old and firmly held Greek tradition relates that the Dorian tribes swept into the Peloponnese from the north in the latter part of the second millennium and thence penetrated to Crete and the Dodecanese, only touching the fringe of the islands in the central Aegean. This is all in accordance with the linguistic evidence that survives. But the central part of the Peloponnese was not affected by this invasion; some of the displaced population took refuge in mountainous Arcadia and there preserved their ancient tongue. What is of special interest and importance is that this language, the Arcadian dialect, is closely akin to that which was spoken in far-off Cyprus and, as will be shown later, this island came within the sphere of Mycenaean influence from the fourteenth century onwards. There is a strong probability therefore that Arcadian is a survival of the earliest form of the Greek tongue, the Mycenaean language.

Fig. 3

The origins of Greek, then, can be traced back as far as the fourteenth century with a fair degree of certainty and, as the archaeological record shows no decisive break in culture till the nineteenth century, it is generally accepted that a population speaking an Indo-European dialect started to percolate into Greece from that time onwards; but the problem of the origin of this people still remains. Two theories are current. One of these suggests that they came from the north through the Bal-

Fig. 3. Greek dialects about 400 BC (*after Wace and Stubbings*)

kans but, if so, they have left no trace of their passage and northern traits in their culture are negligible. The other, more
plausible, theory would derive this people from the East and
across the north Anatolian plateau to Troy, and a grey ware
somewhat akin to Minyan is known in north-east Iran. The
invaders brought with them a new instrument of war, the
horse, which no doubt was a decisive factor in their conquest.
Bones of horses are found for the first time in Troy VI along
with Minyan ware and it is probable that the wave of invaders
that passed into Greece introduced the horse there also. But it is

25

maintained that the transport of this animal across the difficult straits between Europe and Asia would have been a hazardous, if not impossible, operation. For that reason an alternative land route has been suggested via the Caucasus and the north coast of the Black Sea. The fact is that we cannot be sure at this stage whence the Greeks came and by what route they entered Greece, or whether they came by land or sea. Minyan ware is found as far north as Greek Macedonia and Chalcidice but not in Thrace. It is known from most sites on the mainland and from some of the islands in the Aegean.

The conquest of Greece was no doubt a lengthy process, accomplished by several waves of invasion and extending over a long period of time; the mountainous terrain would ensure that. Pillage and arson followed in its wake but not all Early Bronze Age sites were destroyed and nearly all of them were reoccupied. During the next two centuries or so the invaders consolidated their position, absorbed and reintegrated the existing culture, and increased in wealth and power, to which overseas trade and piracy contributed. In the early part of the sixteenth century there is increasing evidence of the civilizing influence of Crete on their culture and what is known as the Mycenaean Age may then be said to have begun. The Mycenaean kingdoms as remembered and described in the *Iliad* start to take shape: Iolkos in Thessaly, Thebes and Orchomenos in Boeotia, Athens (though a very minor kingdom) in Attica. But the greatest concentration of Mycenaean power was in the Peloponnese with Pylos ruling Messenia, and the assemblage of strongholds in the Argolid dominated by Mycenae. Laconia, which lies in between these two, has been little explored and its Mycenaean capital has not yet been discovered. All these kingdoms, it should be noted, occupy fertile plains or uplands, the few that Greece has to offer; and they are separated from one another by high mountain ranges, so that communication was sometimes more practicable by sea. The north-west region of

Greece is almost entirely mountainous and it is not surprising therefore that that area plays no important part in Mycenaean history.

In the succeeding chapters an account, necessarily brief, will be given of the achievements of this Mycenaean civilization with a short historical résumé as epilogue; but before the central theme can be broached two important subjects, the written sources and chronology, have to be discussed.

CHAPTER I

Written Sources: Linear B and Tradition

CIVILIZATION BY DEFINITION in ancient history means a literate society. Indeed the very complexity of civilized society requires a discipline of records to function at all. The Mycenaean civilization was no exception to this rule, though earlier excavations had provided little evidence of the fact. Some knowledge of writing was inferred from curious signs painted on a certain number of Mycenaean stirrup-jars found at Mycenae, Tiryns, Eleusis, Orchomenos, and Thebes; but not until the excavations, begun at Pylos in 1939, produced hundreds of clay tablets inscribed with a similar script was it realized that the knowledge of writing may have been general and widespread in Mycenaean Greece. These clay tablets were not unique. They had already been found in Crete at Knossos as early as 1900 by Sir Arthur Evans, who from the first recognized their importance. Knossos has produced the largest number of such records, between 3,000 and 4,000, though many of them are fragmentary; but they have also been found elsewhere in that island in the palaces of Phaistos, Hagia Triada, and Mallia. Pylos has the next largest number, just over 1,200, and each year's excavation on that site produces its annual increment. Mycenae so far has accounted for little more than 70; and the greater number of these come from houses outside the Citadel.

It seems indeed strange that the dynamic centre and inspiration of the civilization, which we call Mycenaean, should have produced so small a number. The explanation seems to be twofold: the perishability of the substance and perhaps the inability of the earlier excavators to recognize these rather undistinguished lumps of clay for what they were. The latter explanation is a fairly common one given by modern archaeolo-

gists, but I do not think that all tablets could have escaped the
keen eye of Schliemann who prided himself upon the care
with which he collected and preserved what, even to him, were
the most insignificant objects. It is true that tablets are not easy
to recognize. The so-called Linear B tablets – the only kind
found on the Greek mainland – are oblong pieces of clay
about three inches in length. Some are much larger and almost
square; others are long, narrow, and tapering, like a palm-leaf.
In the dust and dirt of excavation tablets could be taken for
fragments of coarse pottery, except that one surface to the dis-
cerning eye would display incised markings. But unlike pottery they were not baked in a kiln, which would have rendered
them almost indestructible. They were shaped out of ordinary
clay, inscribed with a record when the clay was still soft, and
then put out in the sun to dry. So long as they were stored in a
dry place they were likely to survive, but once subjected to the
effects of water they quickly dissolved into a shapeless mass.
(This unfortunate fate befell some tablets stored by Sir Arthur
Evans in a shed with a leaking roof!) It is largely due to the
violent destruction of a site that tablets have survived at all.
The fierce fires burnt them to the hardness of pottery; even so,
some of them are rather friable.

Plate 2

Fig. 8

At Pylos the majority of tablets were concentrated in one
area and in the course of excavation it became clear that these
represented the palace archives. They were stored near the entrance to the palace in a small room with low benches that
supported free-standing shelving, or so it could be inferred
from careful observation of the burnt debris filling the room. It
could also be deduced that the tablets were kept in wicker
baskets, as an impression of the wickerwork was preserved on
several pieces of burnt clay found adhering to 'labelling' tablets, that is, tablets stating in an abbreviated form the subject
of the contents. Another type of storage seems to have been
wooden boxes. Within the Citadel of Mycenae no archives

Fig. 33: Q

have been found. A few tablets, eight in all, were recovered in 1960 in further excavation of Mycenaean houses within the Citadel and near the Grave Circle, but they were very fragmentary. The circumstances of their finding suggest that they were but a remnant of a large hoard, which was all but annihilated by the devastating fire that destroyed the buildings in which they were housed. The surviving tablets were found embedded in conglomerate masses of molten stone, brick, and clay fused to the consistency and hardness of concrete. Spattered about in this rock-like, calcined debris were specks and fragments of a reddish brown substance, which could have been potsherds or bits of disintegrated tablets. If the latter, it would seem that the tablets in this case were stored in stone cupboards or containers. The very evident marks of the fire that destroyed the palace on the crown of the Citadel show that here too the conflagration was of equal intensity and violence to the one farther down the slope of the hill. In this manner any archives that may have existed within the palace would have been obliterated or have left so little trace as to have eluded the vigilance of the excavators.

These records in clay from Greece and Crete, and a few from Cyprus, are practically the only written documents that have survived from the Aegean world of the second millennium. It may well be that other media for writing were used, substances such as wood, leather, parchment, palm leaves, or papyrus, none of which would survive under normal conditions. The conversion of the papyrus plant into a very adequate writing material was a specialized industry of Egypt and there is plenty of evidence of trade relations between the Aegean and that country. Writing in clay was the system adopted in Babylonia and neighbouring kingdoms – there the tablets were oven-baked – and an implement with a wedge-shaped end was used to reproduce the cuneiform script (*cuneus* = a wedge). But the Aegean scribe preferred a stylus or pointed tool and it may be that the more important documents were written on other materials more adapted to such an instrument. The tablets, on the other hand, which could be cheaply and easily produced on the spot, would serve for day-to-day business records, and that is in fact what they are.

How do we know this? So much was deduced by Sir Arthur Evans from pictorial signs on the Knossos tablets recognizable as horses, chariots, weapons, etc., but it was not until recent times, 1952 to be exact, that the many attempts at deciphering the script met with success. This was largely due to the genius, brilliance, and application of a young architect, Michael Ventris, assisted at a critical stage of his work by the Cambridge philologist, John Chadwick. To understand this colossal achievement one must appreciate that Ventris was attempting a far more difficult task than the problem that faced Champollion in solving the riddle of Egyptian hieroglyphics or Grotefend and Rawlinson in the decipherment of cuneiform. These early pioneers had bilingual or trilingual texts to help them and at least they knew the linguistic group to which the language belonged. Ancient Egyptian, though much modified, lived on in the Coptic tongue; Assyrian and Babylonian were related, it became clear, to ancient Hebrew and Semitic languages in general. But Ventris was faced with one script alone and without a clue as to what language it might stand for.

Many of course had preceded Ventris in the unrewarding quest. Sir Arthur Evans himself was a pioneer and laid the foundations for future research. He was able to demonstrate the different stages in the development of the script. First, the hieroglyphic signs that are mainly found on Cretan gems and seal-stones belonging to the first half of the second millennium; a few tablets with hieroglyphs are also known. Secondly, a cursive and simplified version of these signs, which Sir Arthur termed Linear A; this was inscribed on tablets (said to be oven-baked), vases, stone, and on bronze. Finally, a later and more advanced script, closely related to Linear A, which he called Linear B. No exact dates can be given for the periods in which these scripts were in vogue, but it can be said that Linear A overlaps the hieroglyphic script and may have started as early as the eighteenth century. It seems to have gone out of use in the early part of the fifteenth century. Linear B, which is almost exclusively recorded on tablets, begins before or just after 1400 BC. The latest tablets can be dated to around 1200 BC. Linear B is the only form of the script known on the Greek mainland.

Fig. 4

In his study of the material, Evans had established certain basic points: that the tablets were lists or accounts, that a numerical system was clearly recognizable, that some of the signs were ideograms (pictures of the objects designated), and that the other signs were most likely syllabic. This last he assumed because he had noted that groups of signs were separated from other groups by vertical strokes; hence each group probably represented a word of so many syllables. Beyond these general conclusions Evans was not prepared to commit himself. Many of his less cautious and immediate followers – and distinguished scholars among them – were to rely too much on guess-work, choosing a language that might be shown to have some affinity with the script and trying to make the two fit. Method was lacking in nearly all these schemes. Without a

🚶	MAN	🧍	WOMAN
🐎	HORSE		PIG
	TRIPOD		CUP
	AMPHORA		SWORD
	SPEAR	⟫⟶	ARROW
	CHARIOT	⊛	WHEEL

Fig. 4. Linear B. Some ideograms (after Chadwick)

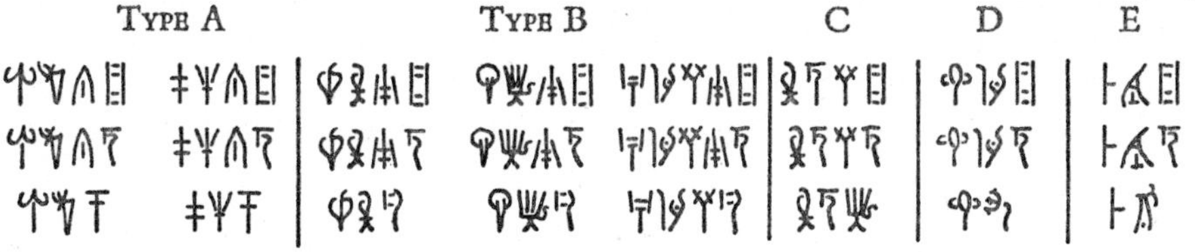

Fig. 5. *'Kober's triplets' (after Chadwick)*

detailed analysis of the inscriptions there was little chance of success. One of the few who adopted a methodical approach was the American, Dr Alice E. Kober. She was able to demonstrate by her analysis of the Linear B signs that it was an inflected language, that is, one in which words have varying suffixes added to denote gender, plural, etc. (as in Latin). For instance, she noted that the totalling formula for men and a certain class of animals differed from that used for women and another class of animals and this suggested a distinction in gender. But her greatest contribution to the decipherment was her demonstration that certain words made up of two, three or more syllabic signs could have two variants by adding a different sign or by changing their terminal sign into another sign. (An example in English would be: wo-man; wo-man's; wo-men). Such variations are referred to in linguistic circles as 'Kober's triplets'! Professor Emmett L. Bennett, Jr was also one of the few to use a methodical approach. Apart from elucidating the system of weights and measures used in the script, his most important contribution was the ordering and classification of the whole Linear B signary. The division of the signs into two classes, ideographic and syllabic, was clarified and from a detailed study of variants in the orthography (bad handwriting is nothing new) he was able to narrow down the number of syllabic signs to just short of 90.

There was one valuable, but deceptive, clue to attacking the problem of decipherment. A related script is found in Cyprus and is referred to as Cypro-Minoan. Only a few tablets have been found there, of which the oldest is said to date from the

Fig. 5

early fifteenth century and has affinities with Linear A. Two features about these tablets call for special comment. A blunted stylus was used and the tablets were baked in fire. The technique is therefore different from the tablets we have been discussing and is more closely linked to that of the civilizations to the East. This is not surprising in view of the geographical position of Cyprus. Yet another script, the Classical Cypriot script, was in use on the island from the sixth to the third or second century BC and is obviously related to Linear B. In most, if not all, cases Greek was written in it; hence decipherment was possible. Seven of the signs are similar to or can be

Fig. 6

equated with Linear B and the phonetic values of the Cypriot Syllabary are known. The signs represent either a vowel or a consonant plus vowel. As this is a syllabic and not an alphabetic script, dificulties occur in words where two or more consonants follow one another or where a word ends in a consonant. Using this syllabic script, '*pastor*' would be spelt *pa-so-to-re*.

The final vowel of *-re* would not be pronounced, neither would the *o* of *-so*; such would be regarded as 'dead' vowels. But the choice of the syllabic sign *-so* (from the five syllabic signs beginning with s: *-sa, -se, -si, -so, -su*) is governed by, and must conform to, the vowel of the syllabic sign following, in this case the *o* of *-to*. So for '*prison*' the spelling would be *pi-ri-so-ne* (the final 'dead' vowel is always *e*). Yet a further complication in the Cypriot Syllabary is that *n* before a consonant is not written. Thus '*contralto*' would appear as *co-ta-ra-lo-to*. It must be clear from these examples that the Syllabary would be a very clumsy method of writing English. It is even more so for Greek. The word *anthropos* 'man' has to be written *a-to-ro-po-se*. Now a very large number of Greek words end in *s* and, as the Cypriot syllabic sign *-se* is identical with one of the Linear B signs, it could easily be demonstrated whether Linear B was a likely candidate for Greek or not. It was found that the *-se* sign very rarely occurred as a terminal sign in the Linear B

Linear B	Cypriot	Value in Cypriot
⊢	⊢	*ta*
+	+	*lo*
⊤	⊤	*to*
⊢ᵁ	⊢ᵁ	*se*
⧺	⧺	*pa*
⊼	⊤	*na*
/ʌ\	↑	*ti*

script. The natural conclusion therefore was that the language was not Greek.

The preliminary, basic, and essential work carried out by Kober and Bennett was invaluable to Ventris who now brought an added dimension to tackle the problem of decipherment, a knowledge of cryptography. In theory any code can be broken provided there is enough coded material to work on. A detailed analysis of the material should reveal certain recurring features and underlying patterns. We have already commented on those that had been noted by Dr Kober. Ventris was able to add to the number of pregnant observations. On the basis of the material available, considerably augmented by the publication in 1951 of Bennett's transcription of the tablets found at Pylos in 1939, he prepared statistical tables showing the over-all frequency of each sign. He was able to deduce – and here he had the collaboration of Bennett and the Greek scholar Ktisto-poulos – that three of these signs were probably vowels from the fact that they occurred predominantly at the beginning of sign groups. A suffix was provisionally identified as the con-

junction 'and', used like *que* in Latin. Other inflexional variations of words identifiable as nouns were noted and, as some of
these occurred with the ideogram of man and woman, it could
be seen that in such cases the inflexion was often one of gender
rather than case.

Fig. 7   The relative accumulated data were arranged by him in
tabular form, in what he called the 'grid'. The grid was constantly being revised and re-arranged. In one of its latest forms
it consisted in the main of 15 rows of consonants and 5 columns
of vowels; as none of the values of the consonants or vowels
was known, these were simply given numbers. Within these
75 spaces were arranged the most frequently recurring Linear B
syllabic signs (51 out of a possible total of 90) on the basis of
statistical data that had been assembled about them. If the
system was sound and the data correctly diagnosed, signs in the
same column should share the same vowel and signs in the
same row should start with the same consonant. Therefore, if
the phonetic values of but a few syllabic signs could be established, the values of the others would automatically follow
from the grid.

We have already mentioned that seven of the signs from the
Cypriot syllabary can be equated with Linear B signs; it was
permissible therefore to experiment with the Cypriot phonetic
value of these signs. This Ventris did. Furthermore, he had
concluded from the constantly recurring position of certain
groups of signs in the tablets that these sign-groups represented
the names of places. Working on these two suppositions he
made tests with ancient place-names. For the Knossos tablets
the choice was naturally made from Cretan names that were
known in Classical times or mentioned by Homer – Knossos
itself, Amnisos (a harbour town near by), and Tulissos; and
they could be recognized in the following syllabic spellings:
ko-no-so, a-mi-ni-so, tu-ri-so. These identifications were certainly
valid on the Cypriot spelling convention, double consonants

Diagnosis of consonant and vowel equations in the inflexional materials from Pylos: ATHENS, 28 SEPT.51

Fig. 7. Ventris's 'grid', 28 September 1951 (after Chadwick)

These 51 signs make up 90% of all sign-occurrences in the Pylos signgroup index. appended figures give each sign's overall frequency per mille in the Pylos index.

Impure ending typical syllables before -⟨⟩ & -⟨⟩ in Case 2c & 3	"Pure" ending typical nominatives of forms in Column I	Includes possible "accusatives"	Also, but less frequently, the nominatives of forms in Column I	
These signs don't occur before -⟨⟩-	These signs occur less commonly or not at all before -⟨⟩-			
More often feminine than masculine?	More often masculine than feminine?			More often feminine than masculine?
Normally form the genitive singular by adding -⟨⟩		Normally form the genitive singular by adding -⟨⟩		

consonant	vowel 1	vowel 2	vowel 3	vowel 4	vowel 5
pure vowels?	30.3				37.2
a semi-vowel?				34.0	29.4
1	14.8	32.5	21.2	28.1	18.8
2	19.6	17.5			13.7
3		9.2		3.3	10.0
4	17.0	28.6			0.4
5	17.7	10.3		4.1	10.2
6	7.4	20.5		14.8	14.4
7	4.1	44.0			
8	6.1	6.1		13.5	15.2
9		33.1		32.3	2.4
10	22.2		30.2	3.5	2.2
11	31.2	33.8	34.4	8.3	0.7
12	17.0			37.7	24.0
13		9.4	14.2		
14	5.0				
15	12.6				

(kn, mn) being split into syllables. The *ri* instead of *li* in *tu·ri·so* (Tulissos) was not a difficulty. Ventris had already recognized that *r* and *l* were interchangeable, as they are in several languages, including Ancient Egyptian. One marked difference from the Cypriot is that final *s* is not written. Similarly *l, m, n, r, s* are omitted at the end of a word or when preceding another consonant, and there are other spelling rules imposed by the

decipherment that do not correspond with the Cypriot conven-
tions.

If the results of these tests were promising, they still did not
provide any clue as to the language concealed in the script.
Ventris's own opinion was that the language was Etruscan and
to the very last he tried conclusions in that direction. It was only
as 'a frivolous digression' (his own words) that in the final
stages of the decipherment he experimented with Greek. To
his surprise, with Greek many of the tablets made sense. Ad-
mittedly as many more remained incomprehensible, but if the
language was indeed Greek, it would of necessity be a very
archaic form of the tongue that was recorded in the Linear B
script a full 500 years before Homer – and Homer's Greek is
itself archaic. If the language was Greek, one would expect to
find many of these Homeric archaisms foreshadowed in the
Linear B texts and the fact that this was so contributed very
largely to the favourable reception accorded by the majority
of scholars to Ventris's revolutionary pronouncement. One has
only to recall the contention and controversy that arose over the
success claimed for the decipherment of cuneiform and Egyptian hieroglyphics to marvel at the comparative acquiescence
and applause with which this far more spectacular and con-
troversial achievement was received. Opposition to the claim
there naturally was, but before it could become articulate a
remarkable and dramatic piece of new evidence supervened.

About the same time that Ventris was reaching his solution
of the Linear B problem, a tablet was being unearthed at Pylos
that went far to confirm the correctness of his system. It was one
of about 400 that were discovered during the 1952 excavations.
Early in the following year they were being cleaned and studied
in Athens by Professor Blegen, their finder. He tried out Ventris's syllabary on several of them, and on this one with striking
Fig. 8   results. It was a tablet with an inventory of tripods and various
kinds of vases, some with four handles, some with three, and

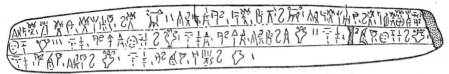

Fig. 8.   Linear B tablet dealing with tripods and vases (after Wace and Stubbings)

one with none; the different ideogram used in every case made this clear. But each ideogram was preceded by a description and, although the meaning of every word in the description was not self-evident, some could be given the following phonetic values – and no other – according to the Ventris syllabary: *ti-ri-po, qe-to-ro-we, ti-ri-o-we, a-no-we*. The *ti-ri-po* word only appears with the tripod sign. Following the spelling convention previously demonstrated, it is clearly the Greek word *tripos*, a tripod. *O-we*, which occurs in the three other words given above, means 'eared'; the word 'ear' is regularly used in Greek for the handle of a pot. It is found above in combination with *quetro* (Greek *tetra*, Latin *quattuor*), *tri* (as in *tripos*), and *an*, the Greek negative prefix, i.e., no handles. That the above-given words should only occur with the ideograms to which they refer was beyond the possibility of coincidence. The basic soundness of the decipherment of Linear B as an archaic form of Greek was thereby established and the publication of this tablet in 1953 served to convince many who up till then were only partly converted. But it did not convince all and to this day there is a small minority of scholars who will not accept the decipherment. Nevertheless, their most distinguished protagonist, Professor Beattie, fully appreciates the awkward implications of the tripod tablet and that it must in some manner be explained away. He has therefore been driven to the desperate expedient of suggesting that Ventris had foreknowledge of this tablet before he arrived at his final solution. Such a suggestion is not only unworthy but completely without foundation.

How is one to explain the opposition, however diminished, to the idea of Linear B being Greek? The objections concern admitted difficulties in translation. Many words still do not

39

make sense and, on account of the great variety of possible alternative readings in certain cases, one cannot always be sure of the Greek form of these doubtful words. It is this very flexibility in the spelling convention that has been particularly under attack. It is argued that no scribe could make himself intelligible to another with such an elastic script. For instance, the sign for *ka* may represent as many as 70 different syllables: *ka, ga, kha, kai, kas, kan*, etc. This is so, but it is not true of all the syllabic signs; and signs are not read in isolation but in combination as words. Certain combinations occur again and again. A pictogram is often there to supplement a hesitant memory. But there are many cases in our own language where we have a choice between variant readings. A word like 'invalid' is capable of two meanings and two different pronunciations, and it is only one of numerous examples that could be given. Like the Mycenaean scribe we may hesitate for a moment before making a choice; it is familiarity and the context that ultimately decide.

If it is generally accepted today – at least by the greater number of distinguished Greek scholars – that the language of Linear B is Greek, it has to be admitted that the written material so far available is limited in quantity and quality. What is the quality thereof? Inventories for the most part and catalogues: inventories of stores, livestock, and agricultural produce; catalogues of men, women, and children. And of the latter category a great part of the text is taken up with proper names and the occupations of the individuals concerned. At least 65 % of the sign groups are proper names, of which a number can be equated with those known in Classical antiquity. About 200 or so are almost certainly place-names, although quite a number of these cannot be identified geographically. Some 3,500 tablets have been studied and these have yielded a total vocabulary of 630 words, of which about 40 % can be read with a fair degree of certainty. The number of texts that contain sen-

tences of any length is limited and consequently our knowledge of grammar and syntax is equally so. These are the
'chariot', 'land tenure', and 'furniture' tablets. It is necessary to
emphasize these limitations in order to retain a due sense of
proportion. The decipherment of Linear B has enlarged our
view of Mycenaean civilization considerably but we cannot always be certain how much of the picture is in focus.

Fig. 53

Before the decipherment of Linear B our only other written
sources of enlightenment on the Mycenaean Age were the
Homeric epics of the *Iliad* and *Odyssey*, and various legendary
tales recounted by Classical and later authors. Many of these
latter accounts were derived at second or third hand and recorded in some cases more than a millennium after the period
to which they referred. But if the Homeric poems were composed in the eighth century BC, as is generally believed, and
certainly not earlier than the ninth, there is a gap of some 400
years or more between one of the principal events of the Mycenaean era, the Trojan War, and the record of it as given by
Homer in the *Iliad*; that is, if we assume that our present version
of the epic is substantially as it was conceived in the eighth
century BC. Even so, there is evidence of at least some later
additions and interpolations in Archaic and Classical times,
though the extent of them is still a matter of argument. If therefore a received text has been tampered with, of what historical
value is the original version – if we could be sure of it – composed many centuries after the events to which it refers? It was
such considerations as these that led nineteenth-century critics
to doubt not only the historicity of the epic but the very existence of Troy. Schliemann proved to them by the practical
testimony of the spade that Troy had existed and had been
destroyed, though he misinterpreted the evidence, and that
Mycenae was 'rich in gold' (as Homer had said), although he
mistook the burials within the Grave Circle for those of
Agamemnon and his followers.

But Mycenaean archaeology was not yet born when Schliemann started his memorable campaigns. Later excavations and
research were to establish a closer relation between the epics
and the findings of archaeology. A tradition that Homer was
born in Chios accords well with the Ionic background of the
epics and it would be natural if his descriptions of warfare and
society were drawn from the familiar life of his own day. Yet
he does preserve features that are true to the period of his tale:
the use of bronze weapons, the boar's tusk helmet that Meriones
lent to Odysseus, the tower shield of Ajax. All of these are
vouched for archaeologically, while the last two can be shown
to have had a very ancient history stretching back to beyond the
beginning of the Mycenaean era, and to have become obsolete
before the Trojan War.

Literary research supplemented the findings of archaeology.
In structure the Homeric poems show obvious resemblances
with the great medieval epics such as the *Nibelungenlied*, *Beo-
wulf*, and in more recent times the Yugoslav epics, which were
orally composed and handed down from generation to generation by word of mouth, or song, and only later committed to
writing. A similar oral tradition can be recognised in the
Homeric epics. Whether Homer was conversant with writing
is a moot point. There is no evidence of Linear B after the
twelfth century and an entirely new form of script, Phoenician-
inspired and totally unrelated to Linear B, did not come into
use till the eighth century BC. But the genius of the epic is not
dependent on writing. It draws its inspiration and strength from
a different mode, the vast reservoir of heroic epithets and for-
mulaic descriptions augmented, maintained, and hallowed by
centuries of oral usage. Some of these can be shown to be very
old on linguistic evidence. Many of the formulas, constantly
recurring and composed in hexameters that are ill-adapted to
the Ionic dialect in which the poems have come down to us,
proclaim their antiquity. And those who created and per-

petuated them were bards who wove them into the sagas that they sang or recited at the courts of kings, extolling the deeds of their royal patrons and those of their forefathers. Of the formulas used the traditional heroic name and epithet was among the most important. Such an epithet as 'swift of foot' applied to Achilles applies to him alone. The two are inseparable. Other examples can be quoted: Odysseus 'of many counsels', Agamemnon 'ruling far and wide', Ajax 'son of Telamon'. And when we find Ajax exclusively associated with the shield 'like a tower', a shield that had gone out of use by the time of the Trojan War, we recognize in him the hero of a saga that is extraneous to, and antedates, the story of the *Iliad*. The same can be claimed for Achilles (a non-Greek name) who, though a minor king, yet dominates the poem and with impunity flouts his overlord, Agamemnon.

Of a different category is the Catalogue of Ships (Book II of the *Iliad*), which at whatever date it was incorporated in the *Iliad* describes a political hegemony of states that was no longer valid after the Trojan War. The Catalogue is an Order of Battle of those who took part in the famous expedition. Mycenae was pre-eminent as leader of the hosts and contributed 100 ships. No other Mycenaean kingdom supplied so many, though Pylos was not far behind with 90 ships. Yet Mycenae had dwindled to an insignificant township in Homer's time and the site of Mycenaean Pylos was no longer known in the Classical period. Athens, of some importance in the eighth century BC, is of small account in the epic. Many cities mentioned in the Catalogue could not in antiquity – and cannot now – be identified. It is also of some significance that Ionia, the home of the two great epics and main source of the local background to the poems, does not figure in the *Iliad* or *Odyssey*; the Catalogue refers to a period before the Greek settlement of Ionia.

Support for an ancient stratum in the Homeric epics is given in indirect ways by Linear B. Some archaic forms of speech in the poems are matched in the Linear B script, but had fallen into disuse in Classical times. Two examples are: the genitive singular in ⁄oio and ⁄ao, and the termination ⁄phi. *Potni' Athenaie* (Lady Athene) recalls *Athana potnia* of the tablets. There are two terms for 'King' in Linear B, *wanax* and *basileus*; in the script *wanax* is clearly the greater title. In Homer the distinc⁄ tion is not so evident but in the Classical period *wanax* was already obsolete and had been supplanted by the lesser title of *basileus*. Many Homeric personal names, but by no means all, occur in the script. Homeric words for weapons incline towards the Linear B rather than to the Classical nomenclature. The relation between epic and tablets is palpable, if superficial.

Although the great antiquity of the epics can be demonstra⁄ ted, it is not easy to disentangle the different periods of composi⁄ tion that are contained in them. The oldest sagas may go back to the beginning of Mycenaean times. Basically the *Iliad* recalls events contemporary with the Trojan War, and the *Odyssey* those of the period immediately following, but centred round the fortunes, or rather misfortunes, of one particular hero. Both poems, however, in the course of their evolution have absorbed other heroic tales and reflect many aspects of the life and cus⁄ toms of later periods. The use of iron (but not for weapons) is mentioned and the rite of burial is cremation, a custom almost unknown in the Mycenaean era but adopted for a time during the Dark Ages that succeeded the fall of Mycenae about 1100 BC. The references to temples seem more at home in the period after the Ionian Migration (tenth century BC) and later. In⁄ stances of the foregoing are rarely recorded in Mycenaean ar⁄ chaeology. On the other hand many Mycenaean features, such as the great vaulted tombs and the wall⁄paintings of the palaces, find no mention in the epics. Lastly, there are alleged interpola⁄ tions and amendments in the poems some of which might be as late as the sixth century BC. But when allowance has been made for all these factors an undoubted historical basis remains.

CHAPTER II

The Pottery and Chronology

THE DATING OF EVENTS in modern times offers us no problems. We have a calendar that has been in existence for hundreds of years; but the further one goes back in time, the greater the complexities that arise, the greater the uncertainties. In Classical times, different systems were used of varying reliability. But going further back still, to the time of the great riverine civilizations of Egypt and Mesopotamia, one meets with increasing problems. There is no fixed date of some great event, like the first Olympiad or the traditional founding of Rome, from which the years may be counted. The only events that were considered of importance were recorded as taking place in a certain year of the reign of a king. At a much later date lists of dynasties of kings and the lengths of their reigns were made, but these were often inaccurate and duplications frequently occurred. The resource of scholars has created order out of the confusing and often chaotic systems, so that there is general agreement to within ten to twenty years for the dating of events in Egypt and Babylonia as far back as 2000 BC. For anything that occurred between 2000 to 3000 BC there is far less measure of agreement and there may be differences of as much as 300 years between the findings of one method of reckoning and those of another. The system of radiocarbon dating (provided suitable samples are found) can hardly help here, as it does not claim greater accuracy than plus or minus 150 years for periods so far back in time.

But how can one devise a system of dating for a civilization, such as the Mycenaean, which can produce no written record of events occurring in the reign of one of its kings and no kings lists? The only answer to that problem is to ascertain what contacts, if any, that civilization had with Egypt and Babylonia, for which a fairly reliable system of chronology has been evolved. Fortunately those contacts existed, but only in a very few cases can a reasonably close date be given to them, and a close date in this context means within 20 or 30 years. The dating of these contacts, however, would be of little value if some form of development within the Mycenaean civiliza, tion itself could not be recognized. It must have a beginning, a middle, and an end and, if further evolution within those three divisions can be traced, so much the better; one can then speak in terms of subdivisions within each group. Such a develop, ment can in fact be recognized in what has survived of the buildings and tombs, and in the many and varied artifacts of metalwork, ivory, jewellery, and pottery. Some evolution, in one direction or another, can be traced in all of them – and it is a correlation of the studies of these progressions or regressions that provides the structure of what is termed a relative chronol, ogy. This would be a flimsy structure indeed and capable of varying interpretations if it was not checked and modified by the evidence afforded by archaeological excavations. Broadly speaking, a succession in time is shown in the construction of one building on the ruins of another. Many such building periods can often be distinguished in one excavation and the true chronological relationship between the objects found in the different strata can be established, those belonging to the lowest stratum being normally the earlier. A similar relation, ship between what is earlier and what is later can frequently be demonstrated in the excavation of tombs.

The most valuable indicator of the passage of time is the potsherd. This humble relic of the past is found in abundance and bears witness to an industry that was one of the mainstays of daily life. Almost alone of all the creations of man pottery has the capacity of resisting time. Clay that is well-fired in the kiln is to all intents and purposes indestructible. More than any other objects surviving from the past, pottery exhibits changes in style, particularly when it is decorated. Because of its fragility it was constantly being broken. The broken piece, the potsherd, can therefore be regarded as almost contemporary with its production. Such a claim cannot always be made for the complete vase, and still less for any objects of obvious value like jewellery, which could so often be heirlooms. Likewise, tools and weapons are unreliable for dating, because they show little change in design over a period of decades.

Before we can approach the established chronologies of Egypt and Babylonia for guidance, it will be necessary to bring some order into the Mycenaean ceramic household. A definite change in the pottery style can be discerned at the beginning of the Mycenaean era, and this provides a convenient point to differentiate it from the preceding age, known as the Middle Helladic period. Similarly, the end of the era is signified by the introduction of an individual type of pottery called Protogeometric. The use of these terms calls for some explanation. As there is no absolute chronology for any area in Europe before the Classical period, a system of relative chronology had to be devised and this has been based on the observed succession of the use of various basic materials in the history of mankind, namely, stone, bronze, and iron. This system is not altogether satisfactory but it has become hallowed by long usage. The Stone Age (Neolithic) of Greece concerns us only indirectly. The Bronze Age can be divided into three periods based on three manifestly different styles of pottery. To distinguish the Bronze Age of peninsular Greece – or Hellas, as it is called by the Greeks – from Bronze Ages in other areas, it is called Helladic. The three divisions are therefore known as Early, Middle, and Late Helladic (hereafter frequently abbreviated to EH, MH and LH). It is with the Late Helladic (the Late Bronze, or Mycenaean) Age, that we are concerned. The Classical period falls within the Iron Age and it is preceded by the Geometric period (its name betraying the style of pottery used to

define it). The beginning of the Iron Age is generally identified
with the Protogeometric period, although in fact a little iron
was already in use at the end of the Bronze Age.

The wealth of archaeological material from the Late Helladic period is considerable and in excess of anything found in the
preceding Early and Middle Helladic periods. Different styles
of pottery can be clearly distinguished, and it is therefore possible to subdivide the period into three sub-periods known as
LH I, II and III (or Mycenaean I, II, and III). The last sub-
period is more abundant in material than those that go before it
and permits of further sub-division into LH III A, IIIB, and
III C. A similar system of relative chronology has been worked
out for the areas bordering on the mainland to the south and to
the east, namely, Crete and the Cycladic Islands. Their Bronze
Ages are referred to respectively as Minoan (from Minos, their
legendary king) and Cycladic. These are divided into three
periods, which are more or less contemporary with those on the
Greek mainland, and the Late Minoan Bronze Age is sub-
divided into Late Minoan I, II and III (LM I, II, III), sub-
periods that correspond in time very closely to LH I, II, III.

To understand the development in style in Mycenaean pottery it is necessary to have some knowledge of that which immediately preceded it and from which it derived, that is to say,
the pottery in vogue during the last phase of the Middle Helladic period. One class of vases of that period is known as Matt-

Fig. 2a

painted Ware, matt paint being used on a light background;
the patterns were predominantly geometric in inspiration. Lus-
trous paint of a red or black hue is substituted for matt paint
towards the beginning of LH I, the patterns become less formal,
and fresh designs and a naturalistic element are introduced. This
change in style is clearly to be traced to Crete. The forms of the
vases mostly follow the Middle Helladic tradition, but new
types are added to the repertory; conspicuous among these is the

Plate I

alabastron. This vase takes its name from a bag-like type of vessel manufactured in Egypt in alabaster. The Mycenaean vase is a squatter, and more elegant, version in clay and can claim descent from the Middle Helladic squat one-handled jar. The Mycenaean alabastra were exported to Egypt and Syria. Such vases found in those countries therefore provide important dating evidence, which will be considered later. This type of vessel was never popular in Crete except to a limited extent round Knossos.

Another vase that was exported to Egypt and which occurs in a reliably datable context there is the so-called Vapheio cup (named after the village, just south of Sparta, near which the famous gold cups were found). The terracotta version of this cup has a long Cretan history dating back to early Middle Minoan times (*c.* 2000 BC). Copies of it in Greece start to appear towards the end of the Middle Helladic period (seventeenth/sixteenth centuries) and their metallic derivation is already apparent in the modelling. The Vapheio cup represents one of the commonest types of vases in use during LH I and II.

Plates 3, 4

In LH II Mycenaean pottery is still strongly influenced by Crete. The inspiration is freer and more abandoned, and it is the great age of the Palace Style Jar, so called from large but elegant storage-jars, decorated in a florid style, that were the fashion at the Palace of Minos at Knossos in LM II. Although these jars originated at Knossos, they were more popular on the Greek mainland and were also produced there. Greece was learning much from Crete, but already at this period the native genius felt sufficiently confident of itself to give its own individual form to the influences that it had absorbed. The Ephyraean style is an example of a disciplined treatment of a familiar Minoan motive; a somewhat stylized flower painted on both sides of the vase which was usually a kylix. ('Ephyraean' takes its name from Ephyra, a legendary city founded by Sisyphos of Corinth. Vases of this style were first found in the presumed region of this city.) The Mycenaeans had inherited from their

Plate 6

Fig. 9

Fig. 9. *Ephyrean goblet (after Wace and Stubbings)*

Middle Helladic forbears this form of goblet and it remained popular with them throughout the whole of their history. It underwent various changes in style but remained essentially the same, a stemmed bowl. In the early stages it naturally resembled its Middle Helladic parent, a deep bowl with a very short stem on a pedestal. In succeeding periods the bowl becomes smaller in relation to the stem and in the final phase the slender stem is often as tall as, and sometimes taller than, the bowl. At this stage of its development it is not unlike a champagne cup. The name, kylix, is taken from a similar, but very much more sophisticated and elegant vase of the Classical period.

The tendency to order and symmetry in design becomes increasingly manifest in the succeeding period (LH III). The old Middle Helladic tradition reasserts itself. Geometric patterns come once more to the fore and whatever is retained of foreign invention is recast in abstract form; and so is born the true Mycenaean rhythm and style, known, admired, and sought after in the ancient civilized world. The forms of the pottery were largely drawn from a well-tried, if rather stolid, Middle Helladic stock, but more elegant shapes and new styles of vases were taken over from Crete, among them the stirrup-jar, which underwent a varied and characteristic Mycenaean transformation. A few examples of this vase had been imported during LH II; in LH III it became one of the most popular

Fig. 2b
Plate 5
Fig. 10f, b

Plate 1
Fig. 10c, d

50

Fig. 10. Mycenaean pottery. a–d, f: LH IIIA; e, g–j: LH IIIB (after Wace and Stubbings)

vases in the Mycenaean repertory. Its main advantage seems to have been the slow rate of flow from the pouring funnel (the side-spout). The jar was produced in all sizes from the large coarse-grained, plainly decorated, vessel used for olive oil to the tastefully painted, smaller model, which probably contain-ed unguents and perfumes.

The standard of production during the LH III period was of the highest order. The clay was selected with care, levigated, and fired to a hardness that gives a clear clink when struck. The pots were sometimes covered before firing with a slip of the same fine clay to make them impermeable. The colour of the vase resulting from the firing was normally buff. Against this background the patterns showed up in a luxuriant paint of red, brown, or black. Almost imperceptibly LH III A merges into LH III B. It is not always easy to distinguish the difference be-tween the two groups, but it is during III B that the Mycenaean style becomes fully established and shows little variation during the whole of this phase. The art of the potter has attained a mechanical perfection and the pottery is mass-produced not only for the home market but for export to the east and central Mediterranean. The vases of this period that have come down to us can be numbered in literally thousands. The repertory includes three-handled jars, stirrup-jars, alabastra (both the rounded and the angular form), small jugs, large bowls (called kraters after the later Classical type), small bowls, kylikes, cups. The decoration, usually a recurring stylized motive, is nor-mally confined to the shoulder or handle-zone on closed vessels. The rest of the vase is painted with bands of circumcurrent lines enclosed by horizontal stripes above and below; this is a conventional form of subsidiary decoration used very widely on Mycenaean pottery of all shapes and is easily recognizable. On open vessels the pattern is usually applied on the upper half of the vase. On certain kylikes the design takes a longitudinal form and occasionally one motive of this nature is selected,

Plate 1

Fig. 10

elaborated, and executed with great skill and artistry on the front and back of the goblet. It is known as the Zygouries style from the site where it was first discovered. In the latter part of IIIB kylikes are as a rule undecorated. At the same time the so-called deep bowl, which starts at the end of IIIA, is increasingly favoured, particularly at Mycenae. Two kinds of decoration are normally found: one of great economy consisting of a simple geometric motive placed sparingly round the central part of the bowl; the other, a panel style, that is, both sides of the bowl between the handles were divided into panels or metopes. The decoration is almost exclusively geometric. Panel style or deep bowls are noticeably rare at Pylos. At Mycenae they occur more frequently on habitation sites than in tombs. Besides the patterned vases, a considerable number – and at Pylos by far the greatest number – were unpainted or at most decorated with plain horizontal bands. Amphorae, hydriae (water-jugs), and jugs were often treated in this manner.

One type of vase was especially popular in Cyprus and is more frequently found there than anywhere else. The earliest examples belong to LH III A. It is a krater painted on the

Fig. 11. Undecorated amphora (after Stubbings)

Plate 5

Fig. 10j

Fig. 11

Fig. 12. LH IIIB krater from Cyprus (after Wace and Stubbings)

53

Fig. 12

Fig. 13

Fig. 14

outside with vivid, though stylized, scenes, commonly of chari⁄ots being driven to the chase or to war. Other popular subjects are fighting bulls, juxtaposed deer or birds, and other more formalized scenes. The antithetical subjects show obvious Eastern Mediterranean influence and these vessels were cer⁄tainly exported to countries near Cyprus such as Syria and Palestine. Another vase that was also favoured in Cyprus – ori⁄ginally of Near Eastern derivation – was the pilgrim flask.

Mycenaean III C pottery is primarily represented by two dis⁄tinct types of decoration, the Close Style and the Granary Style, but there is also a transitional phase following on III B which cannot be clearly defined. The Close Style has been called the III C Palace Style and justifiably so. As its name implies, every available space is filled with some pattern, often of a complicated and finical character. The Granary Style, so called from the large number of pots with this type of decora⁄tion found when excavating the Granary at Mycenae, is the antithesis of the Close Style. Decoration is kept to a minimum. The simplest motives are used, very often one or two wavy lines only. Large parts of the vase are painted in one colour, usually black or brown; sometimes the whole of the pot is painted, leaving but a reserved, horizontal band in the middle that may or may not be filled with some simple geometric motive. The origins of the succeeding Protogeometric pottery are here fore⁄shadowed. Kraters and deep bowls occur very frequently in

Fig. 13. Pilgrim flask (after Stubbings)

Fig. 14. LH IIIC bowl of 'Close style' (after Wace and Stubbings)

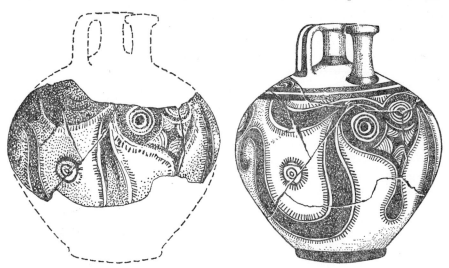

Fig. 15. Fragment of 'Close style' stirrup jar from Taranto, and restored design

the III C repertory and they are painted in both styles. A famous
krater belonging to this period is the 'Warrior Vase'. Towards
the end of the period the quality deteriorated, the brushwork
was often careless, and the paint is notable for its metallic lustre.

Plate 7

During this period (LH III C) local characteristics in style,
scarcely noticeable earlier, become more marked and in this
connection particular mention should be made of a type of vase
produced in the island of Rhodes. Its inspiration was Cretan.
A motive popular in Late Minoan art was the octopus. Many
stylized versions of this denizen of the deep were created, but it
is in Rhodes that the most complete examples are to be found.
A stylized octopus is represented in a rather terrifying but decorative attitude putting forth its tentacles into every vacant surface
of a stirrup-jar; a true enthusiast of the Close Style. Like the
Chariot Vases, these stirrup-jars (the octopus is almost exclusively confined to this type of vessel) had a wide distribution.
They were accepted on the mainland and reached even as far

Fig. 15

55

Fig. 16. 'Incense burner' from Rhodes (after Ventris and Chadwick)

Fig. 68

afield as south Italy. Another product of Rhodes was also exported to south Italy, a perforated vessel of coarse clay on three legs ending in scrolls. It is a common type of Mycenaean vessel (sometimes called an 'incense burner'), but only in Rhodes are the legs treated in this peculiar manner; normally the legs end in straight stumps.

The successive styles outlined in this very brief summary of Mycenaean pottery provide the framework of a relative chronology which at some points can be linked with the absolute chronologies established for Egypt and Mesopotamia. The first point to fix is the beginning of the Mycenaean Age, which in terms of pottery styles is the transition period between MH and LH I. Here we have to rely primarily upon the relations between Minoan Crete and Egypt at this stage of history. In Crete a statue-base and other objects of the Hyksos period were found in association with Middle Minoan III pottery (corresponding with the end of Middle Helladic). The Hyksos domination of Egypt was brought to an end with the establishment of the XVIII dynasty by Ahmose I in about 1570 BC. MM III (the end of MH) can therefore be placed earlier than this date. In the tombs of User-Amen and Rekhmere who were buried in the reign of Thothmes III of the XVIII dynasty, that is, during the first half of the fifteenth century, Minoan envoys – the men of Keftiu (the Egyptian word for Crete) – are depicted bearing 'gifts' to the Pharaoh. Many of these 'gifts' are easily recognizable as metal prototypes of clay vases that were being produced at Knossos and Mycenae during LM II and LH II but not thereafter. It can be accepted therefore that LH II pottery was already being made during the first half of the fifteenth century. Consequently LM I and LH I pottery styles must come between the early fifteenth century and the end of MM III and of MH, that is, somewhere after 1570 BC. A round figure date of 1550 BC is thus normally given for the start of LM I and LH I.

Egypt also provides a date for the LH III A style of pottery. The 'heretic' Pharaoh Akhenaten moved his residence from the XVIII dynasty capital of Thebes to a spot further down the Nile, the modern village of Tell el-Amarna. There he built a new city and encouraged artists from all lands to contribute to its embellishment. But his reign was short, his memory follow-ing his death was execrated, and his capital abandoned. It was not in existence for more than ten years (*c.* 1360–1350 BC) but during that period a quantity of Mycenaean pottery of advanced LH III A style was imported. It is clear that none of it can be later than 1350 BC. III A pottery, though in much smaller quantities, has also been found at Qatna on the Upper Orontes (Lebanon). This site was destroyed by the Hittites in 1375 BC. III A pottery consequently was being produced and exported before that date. When the civilization of Knossos was des-troyed the LM II style of pottery was already giving way to LM III A, the early style of which is closely parallel to LH III A. The destruction of Knossos has therefore to be placed before 1350 BC and the round figure of 1400 BC is usually assigned to this event, but it should be emphasized that this date is only approximate.

The end of LH III A and the beginning of LH III B is ap-proximately determined by another site in Egypt. Pottery that shows elements of both III A and III B styles has been found at Gurob in the Fayyum in association with Egyptian objects that were in fashion not long before Rameses II came to the throne in 1290 BC. Hence a convenient figure for the start of III B is 1300 BC. The end of this period is not so easy to determine, as the traditional III B style may have lasted longer in some areas than others. However, the III C style very noticeably influenced Philistine Ware and it is known that the Philistines were es-tablished in Palestine in the early part of the twelfth century. A round date of 1200 BC is therefore generally accepted for the end of III B.

Egypt	Crete	Date BC	Greek Mainland
III/VI Dynasties 2686–2181	Neolithic		Neolithic
↓	EMI	2500	EH
	EMII	2300	
	EMIII	2200	↓
Middle Kingdom 2133–1786	MMI	2150	MH
↓	MMII	1900	
	MMIII	1700	↓
New Kingdom 1567–1080 Thothmes III	LMI	1550	LH I
1490–36		1500	LH II
	LMII	1450	
Akhnaten 1367–50	LMIII A	1400 (Destruction of Knossos)	LHIII A
Rameses II 1290–24	LMIIIB1	1300 (Fall of Troy)	LH IIIB
Merneptah 1224–14	LMIIIB2	1200	LH IIIC
		1100	sub-Mycenaean
↓ *Late New Kingdom* 1080–664		1050	Protogeometric
		950/700	Geometric
↓		776	First Olympiad
		700	Archaic
XXVI Dynasty (Saite Period) 664–525			↓
Late Period 525–332		500	Classical
		323	Hellenistic
		133	Roman occupation

Before 1550 BC the dates are very uncertain

The Fall of Troy comes within the IIIB period, for excavation has shown that IIIB pottery was still being imported there after the destruction of the city. The Greek historian, Eratosthenes, arrived at a date, in our terminology, of 1183 BC for the Fall of Troy, but his calculations, based partly on tradition and partly on Spartan king lists, are not sacrosanct and recent research inclines towards a date of 1250 BC. This problem will be discussed more fully in the last chapter.

There is even greater uncertainty over the end of LH IIIC, and therefore of the final close of the Mycenaean Age. But this was a period of decline, the beginning of a Dark Age, and information about it is naturally meagre. The start of the Protogeometric period is variously dated between 1050 and 1000 BC, depending on the interpretation of evidence which is outside our subject. Between the end of IIIC and the beginning of the Protogeometric there is a noman'sland, where the pottery partakes of both styles, and this is called subMycenaean. Quite arbitrarily it is allowed a period of fifty years. On such a basis the end of IIIC and of the Mycenaean Age is 1100/1050 BC. The result of our findings may therefore be set out in round figures as shown in the table opposite. For the sake of completeness the approximate dates of the ages preceding and succeeding the Mycenaean are also included.

Chapter III

Religion and Burial Customs

IF ONE WERE TO RECONSTRUCT the Christian religion from the archaeological record, that is, from bare surviving ruins consisting often only of foundations, scraps of frescoes, fragments of mosaics, an occasional inscription, broken objects used in the cult, how valid would be the picture so obtained? Even should a varied but incomplete selection of writings, texts, rubrics, and the like survive to supplement the material side, how much agreement would there be in the interpretation of such documents? To some students of comparative religion there seems to be an obvious connection between the Mother of God and the Mother Goddess of the Eastern Mediterranean; between the death and resurrection of the God-man, Jesus Christ, and the perennial sacrifice of the 'divine son' of the Mother at winter and his rebirth at the spring equinox. A superficial resemblance there indeed is – and this did not go unnoticed in ancient times – but any deep and serious study of the Christian literature will reveal the fundamental difference in concepts between Christianity and other 'similar' religions. With what diffidence must one therefore approach the Mycenaean religion, of which we have but negligible written records and ones that throw no light on the beliefs held! Our main source of information is purely external: shrines, figurines, objects of stone or bronze used in worship, seal-stones and signet rings engraved with religious symbols or depicting some scene of ritual, fragments of frescoes and sometimes pictures on vases, a stele or painted slab telling a similar story. All these are not only difficult to interpret; they are but outward representations and their inner meaning can never be known with certainty.

From the external evidence one can speak of a Minoan-Mycenaean religion; Minoan and Mycenaean representations of religious scenes are almost identical, the cult objects the same. Divinity in human form is usually portrayed as a goddess; a god plays an inferior role. Some scenes suggest a mystic union between deity and worshipper, others depict fertility rites. Tree and Pillar cults, religious concepts of almost universal validity, are frequently shown. How different by contrast is the picture presented by the Homeric epics. There Zeus is Father of all and supreme ruler. Gods and goddesses are but mortals writ large and differ from humans only by reason of their immortality. Little mystery is attached to them. As exalted beings they stand apart. Yet in the later, Classical period, both facets, or what have been termed the Dionysian and Apollonian aspects, of religion can be discerned: the one basically a chthonic religion with Mother Earth as its primeval source and inspiration – a form of worship natural to a settled, agricultural community; the other, a religion inspired by the sky and its elements, Olym-pian and aloof, the natural encompassment of a nomadic tribe. It is generally supposed that the Minoan religion with its chthonic and mystic overtones was the shared patrimony of the Aegean before the advent of the Greeks, and the newcomers adopted the old established forms while preserving their own heritage of Indo-European beliefs. The Greeks by tempera-ment were not averse to foreign ideas. Their genius was to absorb them and to give them new life and character. But in the beginning it would seem that, outwardly at least, the 'es-tablished' religion held sway.

Fig. 23
Plate 8

Relations between Crete and the lands bordering the Eastern Mediterranean were close from an early time, and the Myce-naeans had many trade contacts with those countries in the days of their hegemony. It is only natural therefore to suppose that Minoans and Mycenaeans alike shared the conception of a Mother Goddess and her divine son, and sometimes consort, who is fated to die or be sacrificed at the death of the old year, which he symbolizes, and to be reborn in the spring. The rebirth

Plate 10

was celebrated with great solemnity accompanied by fertility rites that were often of an orgiastic nature. Closely connected with this belief is the *Hieros Gamos*, the divine union of the goddess and her consort, enacted by human agents, to give sacramental effect to the regeneration of Nature. There is enough evidence to show that such practices and beliefs formed part of the content of the Minoan religion, but that it was its central core is doubtful. In Crete the Mother Goddess is a composite character. She incorporates within herself all aspects of Nature from the cradle to the grave. She presides over the birth of a child as Eileithyia and also under many other names. She is worshipped on the mountain peaks as Mother of the Moun-

Fig. 17

tains and a well-known seal from Knossos portrays her standing on a peak accompanied by two lions, one on either side of her, reminding us that she is also Mistress of Animals, the wild ungovernable forces of Nature. Another facet of Nature is vegetation and it is probable that she became fused (or confused) with the goddess of the Tree cult. In another aspect she was the

Plate 11

patroness of marriage and as the Snake-goddess she presided over the home. Again, as Mistress of Animals she had power over life and death. If the general evolution in religion is from the many into one, she represents that process, but some scholars suggest the reverse development; certainly in Greece by Classical times one finds a multitude of gods and goddesses, each with their well-defined spheres, ruled over by all-powerful Zeus, who in Crete, in his Minoan form, was nevertheless subject to the all-powerful Mother.

This dual aspect of Zeus gives us perhaps some insight into the different concepts behind the two religions and their interaction upon one another. Ancient religious systems are not as a rule intolerant or exclusive; more often than not a syncretism is sought. It would be natural therefore for the Mycenaeans to identify their supreme deity with the principal god of the Minoan pantheon even if this involved diminished status and

*Fig. 17.   Seal impression from Knossos
(after Wace and Stubbings)*

new and incongruous attributes. In like manner other Greek gods and goddesses came to be identified with Minoan deities or in some cases were derived from them. The Linear B texts afford some help here. Zeus appears once in the Pylos, and several times in the Knossos tablets. Hera, Athene, Artemis, perhaps Apollo (under the name *Paiawon*), Poseidon, Dio-nysus, Ares (under the form *Enualios*) are all mentioned. Unfor-tunately the information about them is mostly concerned with their dues in kind and other taxes, there is little to throw light on their attributes; but it is indeed important to know that their names were already household words in Mycenaean times.

There are three aspects of the Cretan Mother Goddess that stand out more clearly than any of the others; these are her roles as goddess of vegetation, Mistress of Animals, and household goddess. In terms of the Greek pantheon these aspects could be identified as Demeter, Artemis, and Athene. The name of Demeter is thought to occur on one of the Pylos tablets. The association of this corn-goddess with Eleusis, where she presi-ded as principal divinity, is well known and the Mysteries asso-ciated with this sacred place almost certainly derive from the in-digenous religion. Hera, spouse of Zeus and chief goddess of the Argolid, is another form of the Mother Goddess, but by Classical times her august role had declined and she became subject to the Father figure. Artemis is called Mistress of Animals by Homer. In the Geometrical and Classical periods she is frequently represented as standing between two wild beasts that are chained, and therefore in submission to her. This is a familiar scene on Minoan gems. The same goddess appears under many other aspects and it is significant that as Mistress of Nature the Greek Artemis was identified in west Anatolia with the Great Goddess of the Ephesians, in other words, with a form of the Mother Goddess. In origin, then, Artemis was an all-important divinity who suffered an eclipse with the passage of time, a fact that could not be inferred from our knowledge of Greek myth alone. In later times she appears only as the virgin huntress, though retaining her character as goddess of childbirth, and twin sister to Apollo, a relationship that did not exist in the beginning. The household goddess is associated with the snake and the bird (although the latter could also be the epiphany of other deities). She has plausibly been identified

Plate 9

with the shield goddess on a limestone tablet found at Mycenae, and in that capacity her protection would be extended to the Citadel. One is immediately reminded of Athene who in the house of Erechtheus on the Athenian acropolis was associated with snake, bird, shield, and tree, and in the Homeric epics acted as protectress of her favourite heroes on the Greek side.

From the tablets Poseidon, brother of Zeus, would appear to be the pre-eminent deity in Pylos and this finds its echo in Homer where it is related that Nestor sacrificed nine times nine bulls to the Earth-shaker. Poseidon was also worshipped in the form of a horse, a recognized aspect of the fertility-spirit, and it may be that this form was retained from the original nomadic life and home of the Greeks. His association with the sea would seem to be a later accretion. The ecstatic cult of Dionysus flourished in the Archaic period but there was already some evidence that this was but a revival of an ancient worship, a sup′position that is reinforced by the finding of his name on the tab′lets. His original home was in Phrygia and Lydia, and as the Divine Child he was associated with the Great Mother of Asia Minor. The snake is closely connected with the Divine Child and, when one recalls that Dionysus was said to have been buried at Delphi and that Apollo slew the python before he became the lord of the Delphic sanctuary, there is a strong presumption that Dionysus preceded him there. And there is the legend that Dionysus came to Delphi from Crete, the home of mystical religion. But Greek tradition also relates that the Earth goddess, Ge, was worshipped at Delphi before Apollo.

One god who from his fairly frequent representation in the iconography appears to have been of some importance in the Mycenaean pantheon is the Master of Animals. He is the coun′terpart of the Mother Goddess in that role. Professor Nilsson has very tentatively identified him with Apollo, the lord of the bow, the dispenser of death by sickness but also the healer. This duplication of divine roles may have led, in his opinion, to the later, fortuitous twin association of Apollo with Artemis, one of whose original aspects was mistress of life and death.

In contrast to later times the gods were not venerated in great temples during the Mycenaean period. (Very often the place of worship was no larger than a shrine. Even in the great palace of Minos at Knossos the sacred area was but a small private chapel, overshadowed and dwarfed by the stately buildings that surrounded the great courtyard. Its foundations survive and the elaborate and colourful façade can be reconstructed from fres′coes. There were no cult statues, but in the storeroom of the sanctuary were two small statuettes delicately modelled in faï′ence, which some authorities interpret as a snake′goddess and her votary. A shrine of a humbler sort also existed in another part of the Palace but is not contemporary. It is known as the Shrine of the Double Axes and is subsequent to the destruction

Plate 11

Fig. 18

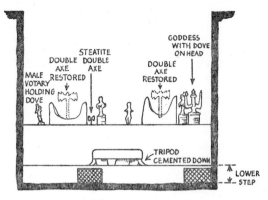

SECTION

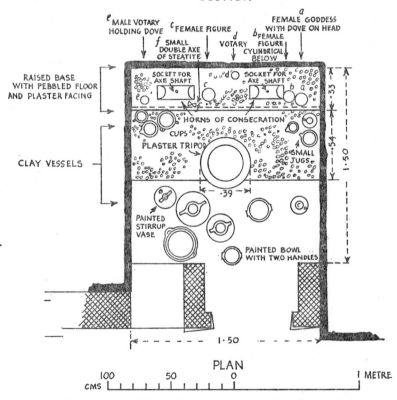

PLAN

Fig. 18. The Shrine of the Double Axes, section and plan (after Evans)

66

of the Palace. Here again everything was on a miniature scale. There were several terracotta figurines of goddesses and votaries (one of which is male) placed on a low dais together with two pairs of horns of consecration of stuccoed clay, each of which may have supported a double axe; one very small stone double axe was found against one of the horns. In front of this dais was a lower one on which rested a round table of offering. On this second dais also and on the floor in front of it were several cups, jugs, amphorae, bowls, and a stirrup-jar for use in the cult.

Many similar sanctuaries are known in Crete but they are rare on the Greek Mainland and only one bears a close resemblance to the Knossos shrine described. It was discovered at Asine, one of the southern ports of the Mycenaean capital, and was situated in a corner of a long two-columned room which was undoubtedly intended for secular use as well. Five female idols and various clay vessels were found on a roughly constructed stone bench and on the floor in front of it. But of greater interest was a fair-sized stone head – of uncertain sex but probably male – and a stone axe of primitive form. It is tempting to recognize the head, if it is male, as representing Zeus and the axe as the symbol of his thunderbolt.

Traces of what are believed to be shrines have been noted at Berbati near Mycenae and at Malthi in Messenia, but there is also evidence that the great Mycenaean palaces had their 'chapels' as at Knossos. From Mycenae comes the exquisite ivory group of two women and a boy. It was found at the foot of the Archaic temple that the Greeks raised to Athene on the crown of the acropolis in the sixth century BC and, as elsewhere we know that Greek temples were built on sites held sacred in Mycenaean times, one must suppose that here also there was a shrine, incorporated into the palace buildings. The two ladies in the group are dressed in elaborate Minoan costume, a fashion that the Mycenaeans adopted almost unchanged from Crete. Some recognize here the sacred triad of

Plates 12, 13

Fig. 19

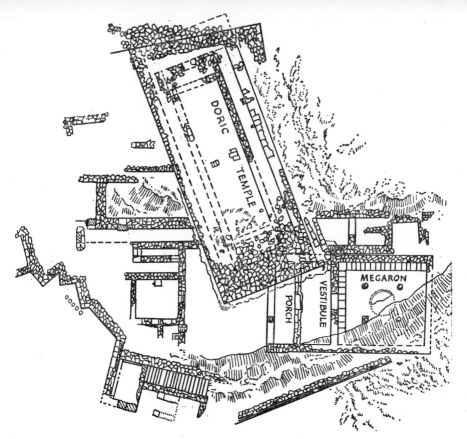

Fig. 19. Plan of the acropolis summit, Mycenae (after Nilsson)

Plate 11

Eleusis: Demeter, Persephone, and Ploutos; others would say they were two nurses and the 'divine child'; others again would claim that they were merely secular. Be that as it may the divinities from the earlier palace at Knossos wore the same sophisticated dress and the perfection in modelling is equally apparent. There is no reason why a wealthy dynasty should not honour its deities with all the artistic ability at its command.

At Pylos a small chamber has been interpreted as a shrine. In front of it in a small courtyard was an altar built of rubble and mud brick, covered with stucco and painted on all surfaces with linear and geometric patterns. But the centre of the cult may well have been concentrated in the private part of the palace itself, the megaron. The focus of the Mycenaean palace was the great circular hearth in the centre of the throne-room. Because of its great size (diameter 4.02 metres) and careful deco-ration it has been thought that it probably had a religious as well as a functional purpose. The hearth played an important part in later Greek religion and was associated with the cult of Hestia. In Crete there was no fixed hearth. In the palace at Pylos miniature votive cups were found on a table of offering in the throne-room and to the right of the emplacement for the throne runs a channel, cut into the floor, that ends in a shallow saucer-like basin. It at once suggests the ritual of libations in which the king would play a principal part, as indeed he seems to have done at Knossos; and although the role of priest-king with its overtones of divinization as understood in Egypt and Babylonia was foreign to the Greek temperament, the combina-tion of the two offices is not to be doubted. A relic of this dual function was perhaps the *Archon Basileus* at Athens in the Classical period. He was an official with priestly functions and bore the title of 'king'.

The sanctuaries that have been discussed above were associ-ated either with palaces or private dwellings. Public places of worship, such as temples, were once thought not to have existed in Mycenaean times, but there are two buildings (and possibly three) at Delos that could be interpreted in this way. They are simple rectangular structures and stand isolated from other build-ings of the period. The assumption that these are Mycenaean temples receives additional support from an important dis-covery on the island of Keos off the coast of Attica. Here an H-shaped building has recently been excavated and in it were found several fragments of cult statues of human size in terra-cotta including a complete head, presumably that of a goddess. There is no doubt therefore that this is a temple. The surface of the head is much worn. It was possibly covered with a white

Plate 14

Fig. 33: A

Plate 19

stucco and painted as in the case of a slightly smaller head of the same material found at Mycenae which resembles it. These are the only remains of cult statues so far known on the mainland, except for the small male head from Asine.

Mention should be made here of the clay figurines that are found in thousands all over Greece and even in areas further afield where Mycenaean influence penetrated. The most frequent subject is a standing woman. Although they undoubtedly have a religious significance there is no agreement as to the interpretation to be placed on them. They are often found with child burials and so some scholars regard them as divine nurses for the protection of the child on its last journey. Others see them as toys, and perhaps the animal figurines (mostly bovine) and stylized chariot groups could be interpreted in that way. But great quantities, and perhaps the larger number, of these figurines occur in settlements. When they are found in sanctuaries one must suppose that they had a deeper religious meaning, particularly those with a more individualistic character such as a seated figure (sometimes represented by an empty throne), a woman carrying a child; and the larger figurines found at Delphi and Epidaurus may have been cult statuettes. The earliest examples known, not many, belong to the first phase of LHIII A. They are abundant in the thirteenth century. They start quite suddenly without any apparent progenitors (Crete being a possible source. Figurines are common there in Middle Minoan, but seem to be rarer in Late Minoan). At first the modelling of them is almost naturalistic. After that there is a progressive development in stylization; the arms that were once modelled free are brought close to the body. In a further stage the upper part of the body becomes a disc, the head an appendage, and the legs a column, so that the shape resembles the Greek letter φ. In the last stage the arms are extended to form a stylized crescent and the shape calls to mind the letter ψ.

Plate 26

Fig. 20

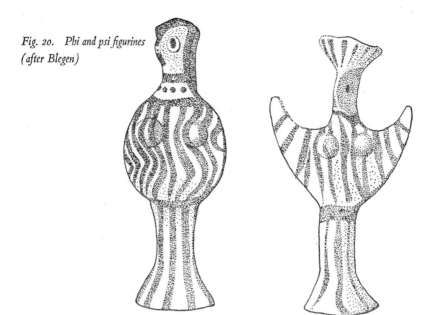

Fig. 20.   Phi and psi figurines (after Blegen)

Besides the palace and domestic shrines there were also rustic sanctuaries. These are only known from representations on gem-stones and signet rings. The Tree cult figures prominently among them and the scenes associated with it can generally be interpreted as vegetation rites. A tree or a sacred bough is often shown within a precinct attended by worshippers, sometimes in calm adoration, sometimes in ecstatic dance. Or a tree may stand beside a shrine and so represent a sacred grove, the seat perhaps of an oracle as at Dodona. The worship of a deity in the form of a column, pillar, or *baetyl* also takes place in rustic shrines, sometimes in association with the Tree cult, but on the Greek mainland the column is more often portrayed as a struc-tural part of a shrine; and in the well-known models from the Shaft Graves of a palace sanctuary three columns are shown in a building crowned by horns of consecration. In such cases the column may stand for the sanctity of the building rather than

Fig. 21

Plate 10

Fig. 22

Fig. 21. Gold-plated silver ring from Mycenae (after Wace and Stubbings)

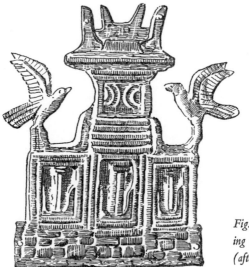

Fig. 22. Gold ornament representing a shrine, from Grave Circle A (after Wace and Stubbings)

Plate 15

a divinity; so also when it is heraldically supported, as in the famous Lion Gate relief.

This dual function, religious and secular, applies to other objects used in the Minoan-Mycenaean religion. Certain vases, notably a particular kind of libation jug shown in cult scenes, may have been intended for ritual use only, but the funnel-

Fig. 23

Fig. 24

72

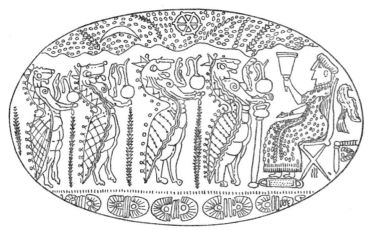

Fig. 23.   Gold signet ring from Tiryns (after Ventris and Chadwick)

shaped rhyton, or filler, certainly had a practical as well as religious purpose; so also the table of offering. Definite cult objects, or rather symbols, are the horns of consecration and the double axe. The former seem to have been a sanctifying symbol. They appear frequently in cult scenes. Placed on altars and on the entablatures of shrines, they enclose within their arms cult objects such as the sacred bough, the libation jug, and the double axe. Many conflicting interpretations are put forward concerning the double axe and none of them is altogether satisfactory. It seems to have had several functions. As a focal centre it may have represented the Mother Goddess. At other times it was a cult implement. Often, like the horns, it was a sanctifying symbol. On vases it was probably decorative, and carved on stone blocks it could be a mason's mark.

The survival of the Mycenaean religion into Classical times is borne out in many ways, but of particular interest is the continuity of habitation at the great sanctuaries, and there is evidence of cult continuity also. The island of Delos is barren and inhospitable, incapable of sustaining human life; yet it was inhabited in Mycenaean times and two buildings belonging to that period may have been temples. Traces of animal

Fig. 24.   LH IIIA rhyton from Ras Shamra (after Stubbings)

73

sacrifices, figurines, and part of a rhyton in the shape of a lioness's head were found beneath the great temple of Apollo at Delphi. No Mycenaean pottery has yet been discovered within the sacred precincts of Olympia but Mycenaean tombs have recently been excavated in the vicinity. Beneath the most sacred area at Eleusis, the telesterion, there was a building of some importance which may have belonged to a Mycenaean prince, and it has already been noted that at Knossos, Mycenae, and Pylos the cult was centred on the palace.

If there is apparent identity in form in the Minoan and Mycenaean religions, there are recognizable divergencies in their funerary customs. Here we are only concerned with those of the Mycenaeans. The earliest graves (late Middle Helladic) are simple and of two kinds: a shallow pit dug in the soft rock and just large enough to hold the contracted body of an individual laid on his side; and an oblong grave lined with stone slabs, known as a cist grave. (Sometimes stones and the rock are substituted for the walls of the tomb and the grave itself may have a covering of slabs.) Usually only one vase is placed with the dead and very often none at all.

A development of the cist grave is the shaft grave, which could reach a depth of 3 or 4 metres. Its most complete form occurs in the two Grave Circles at Mycenae. A layer of pebbles was laid on the floor to receive the body and the long sides of the tomb were lined with low rubble walls that provided ledges for the support of the wooden roof. After the roof had been placed in position, the deep pit was filled in with earth. Sometimes a carved stela or slab was set up to mark the spot. Certain of these graves were intended for a single individual but others are much larger (the largest is 6.4 by 4.5 metres) and contained several burials, all presumably belonging to one family. Because of their rich contents they have merited the name of 'royal' graves. In Schliemann's Grave Circle (now known as A) there were six such graves containing from two

Fig. 25

Figs. 26, 27

Plate 20

Plate 21

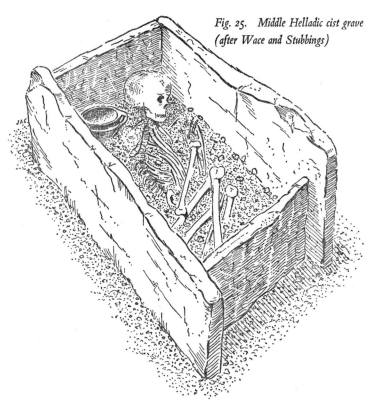

*Fig. 25. Middle Helladic cist grave
(after Wace and Stubbings)*

to five skeletons each. Only Grave II had a single burial. There were also other smaller pit-graves within the circle. In Grave Circle B (see p. 17) there were 24 tombs of which 14 could qualify as shaft graves. The contents of these, though spectacular, are not as rich as those from Grave Circle A; on the other hand B is a little earlier than A and dates from the beginning of the sixteenth century. In both Grave Circles there are instances of extended burial a practice that seems to have started in the late Middle Helladic period concurrently with the increase in size of the tomb. An unusual feature, not found before or after, are the gold masks that covered the faces of some of the dead. Five of these were uncovered in Grave Circle A and one in B. Certain aspects of these royal tombs – the

Plate 16

Plate 18

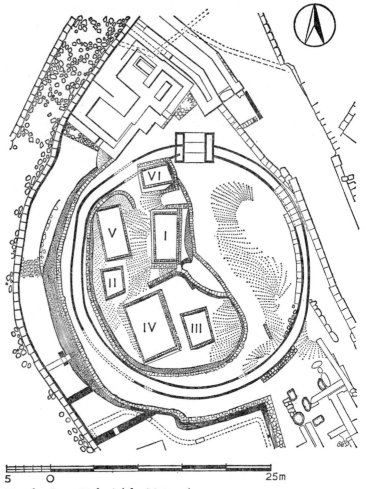

Fig. 26. *Grave Circle A (after Marinatos)*

unusual size of the graves, the wealth and quantity of the funerary goods, the gold masks, and one instance of alleged mummification – suggest that the parvenu Mycenaeans were trying to keep up with the Egyptians, who had set a fashion for grandeur in the Near East for centuries.

Both Grave Circles were part of one great cemetery that reached right up to the foot of the acropolis. Later on in the

thirteenth century, when the defences of the citadel were enlarged, Grave Circle A was still held in such veneration that it
was separated off from the rest of the cemetery and incorporated
within the extended Cyclopean walls at no little inconvenience
to the defence. At the same time a new and more imposing enclosure wall, or *temenos*, was built at a higher level, which en-
dures to this day.

Plate 21

Fig. 28

Nothing really comparable to these grave circles in known
from other parts of Greece, but in the island of Levkas there is a
similar concentration of shaft graves in groups, each of which
had a mound raised over it. They are of about the same date or a
little earlier. Shaft graves are also known from Eleusis and Lerna.

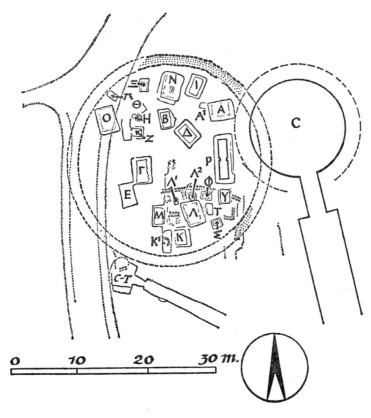

0   10   20   30 m.

Fig. 27.   Grave Cir-
cle B (after Marinatos)

77

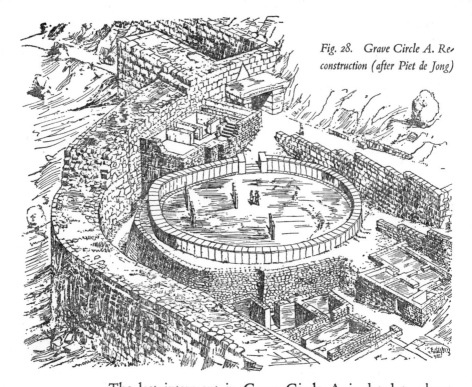

Fig. 28. Grave Circle A. Reconstruction (after Piet de Jong)

Fig. 43

The last interment in Grave Circle A is dated to about
1500 BC but the custom of burial in shaft graves continued to
about the end of LH II (*c.* 1400 BC). Meanwhile an entirely
different type of royal tomb succeeded to the royal shaft graves
at Mycenae. This was the much larger tholos tomb. Round in
plan and shaped like a pointed dome, it is usually built into the
side of a hill (always, at Mycenae). The tholos was approached
by a *dromos,* or long corridor, cut horizontally into the slope of
the hill. (For a more detailed description see. p. 112). The
builders of these tombs at Mycenae are generally referred to as
the tholos dynasty. Nine of these tombs have been discovered
at Mycenae. They range in date from about 1500 to 1250 BC
and show a steady advance in the technique of their construction until the culmination is reached in the magnificent monu-

ments known as 'The Treasury of Atreus' and 'The Tomb of   Plates 22, 23
Clytemnestra'.

Recent discoveries have shown that the tholos type of tomb
is much older than was originally supposed. At one time it was
thought to be later than the royal shaft graves, but only at
Mycenae does this appear to be the case. The earliest example
known is near modern Koryphasion in Messenia. The greater
part of the pottery found in it belonged to the last phase of MH;
it can therefore be dated to the early part of the sixteenth century. Recently another early tholos has been reported from the
neighbourhood of Karditsa in Thessaly. It has the unusual feature that the dromos is partly roofed with slabs. It is stated that
all the pottery from this tomb is MH. Tholoi are found all over
Greece and to a lesser extent in distant parts of the Mycenaean
realm. There seems to be a special concentration of them in the
south-west Peloponnese, though this may be due to the acci-
dent of excavation. The existence of a great many more is sus-
pected.

Concerning the origin of the tholos tomb there is as yet no
general agreement. Circular tombs of one form or another are
found over most of the Mediterranean and even further afield,
but it is not always possible to date them closely. Some of those
in south Iberia are apparently very old, going back into the
third millennium (according to recent carbon dating), but
they are very much smaller than the Greek tholoi and poorly
preserved. Others in the same area approach more nearly to the
Mycenaean form, but are apparently later in date and therefore
possibly influenced by the Greek model. Much nearer home,
the island of Crete had a long tradition of circular tombs, the
earliest of which can also be placed in the third millennium.
Although in plan they are as large as some of the Greek tholoi,
their construction seems to have been entirely different, particularly as regards the roofing, which can only have been of
some lighter material than the stone foundations, such as mud-

brick, wood, or even thatch. Where resemblance between the two types of tomb is close, as occurs in a few cases near Knossos in the fifteenth century, it can be shown that Mycenaean in/ fluence is the stronger. It seems likely therefore that the Myce/ naean tholos was an indigenous creation, in which only cer/ tain features, such as the round plan of the tomb and the cor/ belled method of construction (see p. 111), may have been bor/ rowed from outside.

Little is known about the burial customs in tholoi, as nearly all of them had been plundered in ancient times. A welcome exception to the rule was a small tholos in the vicinity of Nes/ tor's palace at Pylos. Its miraculous escape from the tomb robbers may have been due to an early collapse of the structure (probably in the fourteenth century) and its subsequent loss of identity in later, unsettled times. The tomb, 5.5 metres (18 feet) in diameter, contained a large number of interments (about 23). Four of the burials, the earliest, were placed in pithoi or storage jars; this is an unusual custom that occurs only sporadically in Greece in the late Middle Helladic period but was quite com/ mon in Crete at that time. One of the burials was in a spouted jar of Cretan form. The bones of another interment were placed in a Palace Style jar (see p. 49). This same custom may have been used in a tholos at Kakovatos, some 40 miles further north up the coast. There fragments of several Palace Style jars were found and, scattered about the tomb, a quantity of bones.

The other burials in the Pylos tomb, with the exception of the last one were crammed into pits dug for the purpose. This is a common Mycenaean practice, for where space is limited, there is no alternative if there is to be adequate room for the solemn obsequies of the last deceased. In the present instance the final burial was laid out at full length in the middle of the tomb and with him were placed those objects dear to him in life: a dagger by his left side, an arrow shaft between his legs, a small bronze bowl at his head, a bronze mirror on the lower

Plate 24

Plate 6

Plate 25

abdomen (for mirrors were equally popular with men), and a small vase, perhaps containing ointment, by his side. On his chest there was a bronze awl with an ivory handle, and a female figurine. As none of the pottery from this tomb is recognizably later than the transition period LH II/III (*c.* 1400 BC), this is one of the earliest Mycenaean figurines known.

Plate 26

The grave goods of the pithos burials are interesting. With one of the older jars, painted in a MH tradition, there was a shallow cauldron, a rapier, a dagger, all of bronze; a fragment of a gold leaf circlet was found at the bottom of the jar. With another jar, also painted in MH style, there were four rapiers, two flint arrowheads, and a deep cauldron containing a number of bronze implements. Within the jar and mixed up with the bones were several long bronze pins, perhaps used for pinning the shroud, and a fragment of a silver vessel with a repoussé design. The spouted jar of Cretan design only contained a terracotta cup of Vapheio style, but close by were three rapiers and two daggers. The fourth jar of Palace Style, and therefore latest in date (fifteenth century), contained nothing but the skeleton. Two of the pits for the rejected skeletons were devoid of grave goods, but one of them contained six daggers and three fragments of gold foil which made up into a handsome diadem. It is a very much smaller version of the magnificent examples uncovered in the shaft graves of Mycenae. Many of the weapons, in fact, found in this tholos find their counterparts in the shaft graves. The tomb seems to have been used for about 150 years.

Plate 24

Plate 27

The contents of this tholos have been described at some length because it is one of the few that has escaped comparatively intact. It was not a rich tomb but must have been representative of the status of the princely family living in that district. Two other tholoi that partly escaped the attention of the plunderers give some indication of the great wealth that was deposited in these tombs. One of these at Routsi, not many miles distant from the Pylos tholos, was excavated by Professor Marinatos; as well as a great number of finely carved gems it produced several beautifully inlaid daggers that bear comparison with those found in the royal shaft graves. The other tomb, at Dendra (ancient Midea), not far from Mycenae, was excavated by the Swedish School. Here three of the four graves within the tholos were remarkable for the splendour of their equipment. This tomb also illustrates an apparent distinction in burial custom between the west and east Peloponnese. Although the tholoi around Mycenae have all been robbed and have only the grandeur of their monuments to convey the riches that they once held, they appear to have contained but few burials; in other words, each tomb in the east Peloponnese seems to have been prepared as the last resting place for a single king, his consort, and perhaps a favourite child. An exception to the rule may be the so-called Lion Tomb at Mycenae, where a semicircular pit along the wall of the vault could have contained the discarded remains of earlier burials. In Messenia, on the other hand, the tholoi were family vaults built to receive many generations. At Mycenae no tholoi appear to have been built after the mid-thirteenth century, but elsewhere in Greece they continued in used to the end of the Mycenaean Age, and in Thessaly and Messenia tholoi, though much smaller in size, were being raised as late as the Protogeometric period (tenth century BC).

Only an abbreviated and largely suppositious account can be given of the funerary rites in a tholos at the death of a royal personage. The great vaulted tomb was probably to be seen in all its splendour when it was opened to receive the first royal funeral. If it was held in the Treasury of Atreus, the procession of mourners would move slowly up the long dromos, the walls rising higher on either side of them as they penetrated into the heart of the hill. Before them towered the tremendous doorway with its intricately carved entablature and the tall half-columns

Plate 28

Fig. 29
Plate 22

Fig. 42

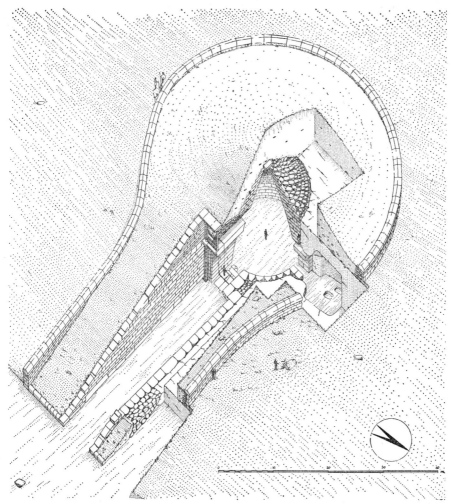

Fig. 29. Treasury of Atreus. Isometric View (after Hood)

flanking the entrance to the tomb. The great bronze doors with their gilded bosses would be swung back to receive the cortège and in the dim light the vault with horizontal bands of bronze would gleam with a thousand gold rosettes. Spread out on the earthen floor was a carpet of gold to receive the body of the king, arrayed in his robes of state, crowned with his diadem, his seals of office attached to his wrist, and his favourite dagger at his side. Around him would be laid the vessels of food, the flagons of wine, jars of oil and unguent, and all the necessities for the sustenance and care of the body on his last journey. Weapons of war would be added too: swords, rapiers, daggers, and spears, the mighty figure-of-eight shield, the well-stocked quiver, and the bow. One rapier has a special task to perform. It is taken from the pile and to the words of a solemn incantation the blade is bent so that its spirit may be released and be swift to do battle for its master, should threatening demons bar his way. Then the signal is given for the slaughter of the horses that had drawn the chariot with the bier, and that have been fidgeting nervously in the dromos, apprehensive of the doom that awaits them. There follows the slaying of the rams and other sacrificial beasts within the vaulted tomb itself. The fires are lit, the sacrifices roasted, and all partake of the funeral banquet. In the still glowing embers the mourners cast their last tributes to the dead, and then withdraw. After the great doors have been closed the masons can begin their work of sealing up the entrance. The mourners would have to tread with care around the slaughtered horses, now carefully laid out to face one another in death; only with difficulty can they make their way through the serried ranks of slaves that line the dromos, and as they come out into the unwonted light they see other slaves silhouetted on the dromos walls and behind them banks of soil. A few large blocks of stone have already been placed in position at the entrance to the long corridor, for the filling in of the dromos is about to begin.

The above is naturally a composite picture embroidered with fantasy, and it embodies customs that were not carried out at every funeral. For instance, we have only one record of the slaughter of horses in the dromos. That was only recently brought to light in the re-excavation of the dromos of a tholos

Plate 29

tomb near Marathon. The episode of the bent rapier was taken from the unplundered tomb at Pylos, and the gold carpet from a plundered one near by.

Second and subsequent burials in the same tomb would have been far less impressive. If the death was sudden and in the height of summer, even a host of slaves working feverishly could not clear the dromos and dismantle the stone blocking wall in time. Instead, the dromos was partly cleared to form a ramp and only the upper part of the blocking wall dismantled. The cortège would have to walk up the ramp and descend by ladders into the tomb. The atmosphere in the vault after a long passage of time cannot have been pleasant. Hastily fires would have been lit and aromatic perfumes burnt to sweeten the air in preparation for the next solemnity. All must be made ready to receive the new burial, and so the remains of the former tenant are gathered together and placed in a hurriedly dug grave near the wall of the vault. A lot of petty pilfering must have taken place during these preparations in which so many people would be busily engaged; and nobody would protest if some members of the family removed different precious articles, which they might claim were once their own. This is to record but human foibles. At an earlier period the sanctity and awe in which the kings of the shaft graves were held was no doubt sufficient to avert such spoliations.

If the second sepulture lacked the dignity of the first, later ones must have been even more macabre. Apart from having to scramble in and out of the tomb, there was an increasing lack of space as each new burial was deposited and former interments thrown aside. Extra pits would be dug or existing pits crammed with the latest skeleton. That is the unpleasant picture left by the little tholos at Pylos. Time has softened the outlines, but the crude reality remains.

The burial customs described above were not confined to royal tombs alone. They were general in all classes of society

Plate 31

Plate 30

85

and throughout the whole Mycenaean age. Only the style of sepulture varied. The poorest section of the community could but afford the simple grave of their Middle Helladic forefathers, whereas for the nobility and wealthier classes burial in a chamber tomb was almost universal.

Fig. 30

The use of chamber tombs starts in LH I and according to some authorities they are copied from the rock-cut graves of the Middle Kingdom in Egypt. In Messenia, on the other hand, some of the earlier examples of chamber tombs are not unlike a small version of a tholos, reproducing the circular form and even the pointed dome. But normally the plan is roughly square or oblong with rounded corners. Like the tholos, it is excavated in the side of a hill and approached by an open corridor or dromos which was filled in after the burial; but the important difference, apart from size, is that no masonry is used except for walling-up the door to the chamber or for reinforcing weaknesses in the rock structure. To avoid the danger of collapse the roof is normally slightly hipped, but this precaution was often unavailing. The walls of the dromos often were inclined inwards, the width of the passage being narrower at the top than at the bottom. This same feature was sometimes reproduced in the doorway which therefore resembled the entrance to an Egyptian tomb. The floor of the dromos sloped down towards the

Plate 32

chamber. In LH I and II the dromos is usually short and wide, its incline steep, and sometimes it is stepped. In LH III the slope is gentle and the corridor could be more than 100 feet in length. ·

Chamber tombs were family burial vaults and, as with the royal tholoi, they were reopened for each successive burial. The deceased was laid in the centre of the tomb, usually on his back, his head sometimes supported by a stone pillow. He was buried fully clothed apparently, as buttons are sometimes found on the skeleton. Apart from personal belongings, the grave furniture usually included a number of vessels, mostly of clay.

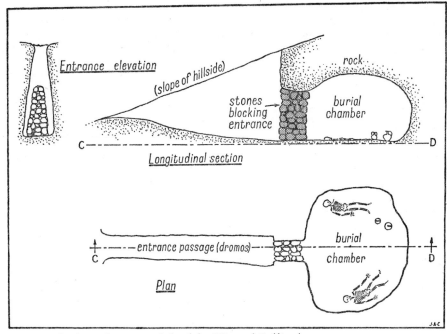

Fig. 30. Chamber tomb. Section and plan (after Wace and Stubbings)

At the next interment he would be laid to one side, if there was room, but as the tomb filled up, the earlier occupants would be disposed of in pits. Sometimes a side chamber, if it existed, would be used as a charnel house. Occasionally former burials were relegated to a niche cut in the walls or a pit dug in the dromos. The most desperate measure was to clear out the whole of the chamber, throw the bones into the dromos, and start afresh. This may have happened in cases where the tomb was taken over by a collateral branch of the family or by an entirely new family. But often nature would lend a hand. In many cases disintegration of the roof laid a pall of débris over the floor and, instead of clearing this away, some families would choose to place the burials on top of this layer. Over a long period of time the level of the 'floor' would almost reach the roof! Such cases provide admirable stratification for the archaeologist

Plate 34

Plate 32

and sound dating evidence. The restrictions of space would not allow an elaborate ritual within the tomb, even when it was new. Some sort of ceremony took place in the dromos, for almost invariably a large number of kylikes (see p. 50), pur- posely broken, are found in the corridor. This suggests that libations were poured to the dead. There is also evidence of a funerary feast. After the last rite had been performed, the door of the tomb was walled up and the dromos filled in. As it would have to be cleared again for a new interment and the wall taken down, it is presumed that a stone marker was placed above the tomb for identification. None have been found, but

Plate 33

in one case at least a small rough pillar of stone was placed be- fore the entrance to the tomb within the dromos itself. It may have signified that no further burials were to be laid there, for the tomb was found intact and it contained but three burials.

The last solemn rites that were performed at a burial are in strong contrast to the callous disrespect shown to earlier inter- ments. Professor Mylonas has advanced a plausible theory to account for this. In his opinion the soul of the deceased only remained attached to the grave so long as flesh and bone stayed together. Once the flesh dissolved the spirit was released from this world never to return to it again. The funerary gifts were partly intended to placate the dead person during the period of waiting. They were also needed for the journey to his final abode; but once he had reached his destination, an event that was signified by the disintegration of the body, both bones and gifts could be treated with impunity. These beliefs are perhaps not so far removed from the later Classical conception of Hades, the melancholy land of shades that knew neither joy nor sorrow, a belief so ingrained in the Greek temperament that traces of it survive even into Byzantine Christianity.

CHAPTER IV

The Houses of the Living and the Dead

The plan of the nucleus of a Mycenaean palace
derives from a Middle Helladic model of uncomplicated
design: a long room, preceded by a vestibule on its short side.
In front of the vestibule of this early model there was no doubt
a porch of primitive construction, such as is found with many
village houses in Greece today; that is, a trellis framework supported on two posts, with a vine or some creeper for shade. In
the Mycenaean palace these features took the form of a columned
porch, leading into a vestibule and thence into the main room
or megaron. Frequently the Middle Helladic house had another
room at the back, which was used as a storeroom and had its
own separate entrance, a feature reproduced in Nestor's palace
at Pylos. A fixed hearth, sometimes round, is usually found in
the living rooms of MH and LH houses. In the Mycenaean
palace it was of great size and occupied the central part of the
megaron. Arranged symmetrically around the circular hearth
were four round column bases, often of a hard blue limestone.
The size of these indicates that they supported tall wooden
columns of great height and strength, sufficient to raise the
central part of the roof above the rest of the room and thereby
create a clerestory. At Pylos the remains of two pipes of a great
terracotta chimney were found above the hearth, but it cannot
be assumed that chimneys were in general use in the humbler
dwellings.

The palace of Mycenae, as head and chief city of all the prin-
cipalities of Greece, would have been the most resplendent of
all the royal residences. But it has suffered not only from the
hand of the despoiler; its superb, commanding position on the
crown of the acropolis has exposed it to the merciless elements
and they have not spared it either. The foundations of the

Fig. 31

Fig. 33: H

Plate 14

Plate 35

Fig. 19

Fig. 32

Plate 36

Plate 37

Fig. 33: E

Fig. 42

Plate 15

megaron, vestibule, porch, and courtyard indeed survive in part, but of important buildings higher up there is scarcely a trace and later builders have stripped every stone to the bare rock to construct an Archaic temple or a Hellenistic house. Tiryns was one of the lesser Mycenaean kingdoms, and yet the grandeur of the palace plan is more to be discerned there than at Mycenae. But for the fullest exposition of residential plan and administrative office one must turn to the palace of Nestor at Pylos.

Unlike the citadels of Mycenae, Tiryns, and Athens, the capital city of Nestor is not confined within the rocky bulwarks of an acropolis. Its defences compared to theirs are minimal. From the sea and a narrow fertile plain the ground rises gradually and not too precipitously to a flat-topped eminence that unobtrusively asserts its superiority over the neighbouring hills. Set back from the sea to avoid surprise attack, the city commanded an extensive view; a great part of the coast to the west came under its eye as well as the hinterland rising to the mountain barrier of Aegalion to the east. The modern approach to the site may not impress the visitor as do the menacing and towering walls of Mycenae and Tiryns, for it is tucked away from the road in an olive grove, now sadly decimated by the encroaching excavations. Only the lower courses are to be seen today, but in ancient times the lofty walls of the palace would be visible from afar. The approach was through a building not unlike the Classical propylon in plan, a gateway with an outer and inner porch, each supported by a single column. As in all Mycenaean palaces and buildings, private or public, the columns were usually of wood and consequently do not survive, but the form of them is known. At Mycenae there was considerable variety. The stone half-columns from the tholoi are either fluted ('Tomb of Clytemnestra') or have a zig-zag pattern (Treasury of Atreus). In the Lion Gate relief the shaft is plain and tapers towards the base (in contradistinction to the

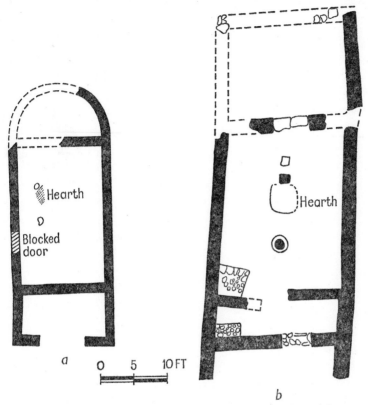

Fig. 31. House plans at Korakou. a. Middle Helladic; b. Late Helladic (after Wace and Stubbings)

column of the Classical orders). This is usually the type that is reproduced in the miniature ivory columns found in the House of Sphinxes. These same ivories show capitals that vary from the simple prototype of the Doric echinus to the elaborate and sophisticated form of the sixth-century Archaic capital from a Treasury at Delphi, which indeed is foreshadowed in the Mycenaean ivory models. Whatever the form of the capital at Pylos, the column-shaft is almost invariably fluted; the number of flutes varies from 32 to 64. This evidence arises from

Plate 45

the continual replastering in ancient times of the collar at the base of the shaft; the perished column has left its impression in the plaster surround.

On the right, as one entered the gateway, was a room that seems to have been for the use of the guard; a low platform immediately to the left of the door indicates the position of the sentry's stand. The rooms to the left of the gateway were for the archives. Here were kept records of daily transactions: the share of produce due in taxes to the royal household, or to the gods: the allotment of materials, man-power, and so on for the many tasks of government. The entrance to the palace was a convenient control point for the execution of daily business. So at Mycenae the Granary by the Lion Gate may have served the same administrative purpose.

If one was an honoured guest at Pylos, one would be taken across the court to a waiting room that was immediately to the left of the porticoed entrance to the royal apartments. Here there was a white stuccoed bench filling one corner of the room, the vertical face of which was painted with some pattern, now mostly effaced. There were also two large pithoi, both of which may have contained wine, for next door there was a pantry well-supplied with drinking cups (kylikes). There must have been a lot of woodwork in this pantry, probably cupboards and shelves, since here the fire that finally destroyed the palace was so intense that it melted some of the pottery to a mass of green glaze! The waiting room, whether wine was served or no, must have been a place of ritual preparation for any guest about to enter the presence. Ablutions and libations would probably form part of the ceremony.

The lay-out of the state rooms shows that they were well adapted both for solemn occasions and for the practical management of everyday affairs. The porch and vestibule were richly adorned with frescoes, and here a favoured guest might be offered rest for the night. 'Nestor of Gerenia bade Telemachus,

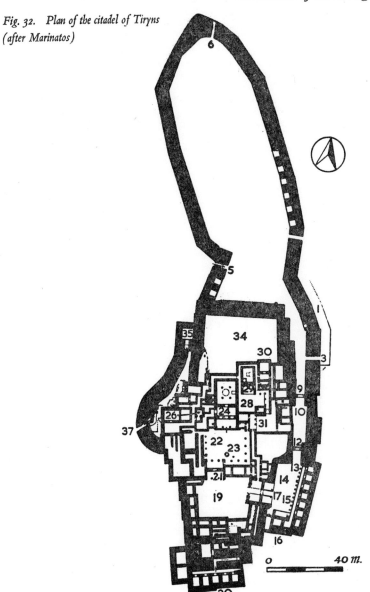

Fig. 32. Plan of the citadel of Tiryns
(after Marinatos)

40 m.

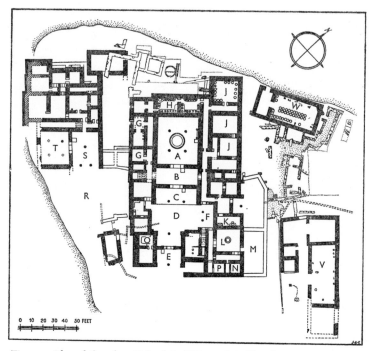

Fig. 33. Plan of the palace, Pylos (after Wace and Stubbings) A = megaron; B = vestibule; C = porch; D,M,R = courts; E = propylon; F = columned porch; G = pantries; H,J,W = store-rooms; K = bathroom; L = queen's megaron; N = boudoir; P = lavatory; Q = archives room.

the dear son of godlike Odysseus, to sleep there on a corded bedstead under the echoing portico.' The contrast on moving from the wide but shallow vestibule into the well-proportioned columned hall of the megaron must have made a deep impression. One's gaze was immediately drawn to the four tall, fluted columns upholding the lantern or clerestory over the great circular hearth with its painted border. The sacred fire, burning low, would add motion to the many coloured spirals that followed one another round the verge in an unbroken ring. We do not know what decoration, if any, was applied to

Plate 13

the ceilings above the aisles, but special care was devoted to the embellishment of the floor. The plaster surface was methodically, but not too accurately, divided off into squares of which the outline was incised; and the squares were painted with various designs. These were usually geometric but one particular square in front of the throne was decorated with a stylized octopus, which was perhaps a royal emblem. The walls of the throne-room now stand but 3 feet high, but when first built their stuccoed surfaces recounted many a saga in brilliant colour of feats of valour and heroic legend, such tales as the king fain would hear at royal feasts from the lips of the bard; and indeed one fragment of a fresco survives to show perhaps the bard himself, lyre in hand, or maybe it is Orpheus charming beast and bird by his music. Behind the throne a different theme is portrayed upon the walls. It is a device of royal heraldry. Two couchant griffins face each other across the throne, proud heads aloft, their wings outspread. Each wears a jewelled tufted crest, peacock feathers adorn the powerful shoulders, and the tails are upraised and curled as if in royal salute. Behind each griffin and in attendance, as it were, is a couchant lion. Might the lions, by some rule of Mycenaean heraldry, represent the arms of a house allied by marriage? Are these the royal lions of Mycenae? And, one might go on to ask, was the house of Nestor related to the buccaneer prince who conquered Knossos and whose royal griffins usurped the throne of Minos? But this is to impose medieval heraldic custom on Mycenaean.

During the day the vestibule, or antechamber to the throne-room, was a place of great activity. It was the corridor through which direct communication might be had with all parts of the palace. Apart from the two great central portals in the long sides of the room there were the doors at either of the short ends. The one on the left, as you faced the megaron, gave direct access to the pantries and crockery-stores, and a staircase opposite the door led up to the second storey. The pantries were an

Plate 37

Plate 38

Plate 55

Fig. 33: G

important part of the palace establishment. In one of them the stems of no less than 2,853 kylikes – all originally stacked on shelves – were counted. The consumption of wine in the palace appears to have been high. The poet tells us of Nestor's golden cup that, when filled, none but he could raise. This cup has not survived, but in his palace have been found two great drinking vessels of clay that far exceed in size the ordinary kylix. One of them has a capacity of ten pints!

The door at the opposite end of the vestibule brought one into a corridor and face to face with another staircase, of which the lower flight of eight stone steps is well-preserved. Turning to the left in this corridor one had access to various storerooms *Fig. 33: H* and to a double room at the back of the megaron, which contained vast supplies of olive oil. The system of oil storage differed from that in the House of the Oil Merchant at Mycenae (see p. 101). At Pylos the pithoi are partly sunk into the ground: the upper half is above floor level and this is encased in clay covered in stucco, which prevented seepage of spilt oil and could be easily cleaned. The pithoi are arranged around the sides of the room, so that in their plaster casings they look as if they were enclosed within a long and broad bench. The containers were very deep and long ladles had to be used to empty the jars when the level of oil was getting low.

Returning once more to the vestibule along the above-mentioned corridor, but this time keeping straight ahead and passing through a columned porch that gave on to the main courtyard, one would reach the queen's apartments. These com- *Fig. 33* prised a smaller megaron with central, painted hearth but without columns, and two small rooms separated by a corridor, one of which from its decoration could be described as a boudoir. Next door to, and to the north-west of, the queen's megaron but not immediately accessible to it was a large bath- *Plate 39* room. The bath itself is of terracotta and enclosed in a surround in true modern fashion, except that it consists of clay covered over with white plaster. A refinement, not found with many modern baths, is a broad step, also plastered, for assistance into the bath; once one was comfortably ensconced therein a ledge at the waisted centre provided a convenient resting-place for the equivalent of a sponge-rack! In the corner of the room are two great wide-mouthed jars, also encased in a plaster-coated surround. At the bottom of the jars there were broken 'champagne glasses' (kylikes), and two similar vessels were also found in the bath. One should avoid jumping to modern conclusions. In some Turkish baths today (in their home of origin) water is poured over the body from shallow vessels not unlike, and certainly no greater in capacity than, a Mycenaean kylix. In ancient times oil, as well as water, would be used for the cleansing of the body. In the *Odyssey* it is related that the fair Polycaste, youngest daughter of Nestor, bathed Telemachus, 'And when she had bathed him and anointed him with olive oil... forth from the bath he came in form like unto the immortals.'

The position of the bathroom in relation to the plan of the palace suggests that it was for general rather than private use. It is much more easily reached from the central court and its rooms than from the queen's megaron, which it immediately adjoins. It would therefore be quite natural and convenient for Telemachus to be conducted there from the vestibule for his ceremonial bath. No comparable bath or bathroom has yet been found on any other Mycenaean site. At Tiryns there only remains the floor which is a great monolithic slab with drilled dowel holes along the edge for the fixing of wooden walls; these, of course, would have been plastered. The floor is gently tilted to allow the waste water to flow towards the drain. At Pylos the bath itself has no 'plug' and the water would have to be baled out and poured away into a drainage conduit passing through the wall.

The central court of a Mycenaean palace must always have presented an animated scene. At Pylos it is smaller than at

Fig. 34. The Great Court at Mycenae. Reconstruction (after Marinatos)

either Mycenae or Tiryns, but its diversity of porticoes and loggias gave it a more varied and unconventional appearance. The largest of the palace courts, that at Tiryns, was much more formal, but its long colonnades of alternating pillar and column must have lent it great dignity. The Great Court at Mycenae was paved with stucco and divided off into squares painted with geometric patterns, but the courts at Pylos had plain cement surfaces interrupted inconspicuously by an occasional drain outlet for rain water. This consisted usually of a stone slab pierced with three holes. Underneath the palace there is a maze of drains not yet fully explored. The smaller ones, built of stone with upright slabs and cover stone, were big enough to allow a slender man to wriggle through. They emptied into much larger drains of like construction in which a man could almost stand up. A similar system can be seen at Mycenae but

Fig. 32

Fig. 34

there the roof consists of two stones juxtaposed to make a pointed arch, the corbel technique. Mycenaean drains were primarily used to dispose of rainfall and any rubbish that was swept along with it. Anything approaching a civilized lavatory must have been of rare occurrence.

Around the great palace complex were clustered the houses as in a medieval fortress town. Those around Pylos have not been investigated to any great extent, and at Mycenae only the basements have for the most part been preserved. Because of the often precipitous nature of the terrain, terraced buildings were quite usual and the most direct communication between one level and another was the stepped street, but the indirect approach by means of a ramp, winding backwards and forwards up the side of the hill, was also used. Sometimes such a road would assume monumental proportions as in the case of the

Fig. 35

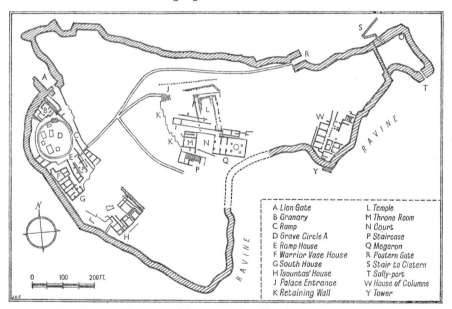

Fig. 35. Plan of the Citadel, Mycenae (after Wace and Stubbings)

Great Ramp at Mycenae, which is supported by a terrace wall
of Cyclopean construction (see p. 110). We may picture Agamemnon driving in his chariot through the Lion Gate – the
threshold still shows the marks of wheels – and up the acropolis
Fig. 50   to the entrance of his palace which was approached by a great
staircase. The first flight of twenty-two steps of this monumental
Plate 41   stairway is still preserved today. The treads of ashen-grey sand-
stone are built on a stone fill. The second flight, parallel to it
and leading up in the reverse direction, no longer survives but
it is believed to have been of wood.

A ramp of some importance skirted the east side of a house
excavated by Professor Tsountas near the Citadel walls. It was a
broad road with a good white plaster surface and there is some
evidence that it was sheltered from the noonday heat by a roof
supported on a colonnade; one is reminded of the porticoed
way leading to the south entrance of the Palace of Minos.
Strategically placed at a bend in the road was a white plaster
bench for the tired traveller. From there one could gaze on the
smiling plain of Argos, on the grey bluffs of the Arcadian hills
beyond, and on the peaceful little villages at the foot of the
acropolis, which made up the capital city of Mycenae.

For the city of Agamemnon, like all the other royal Mycenaean townships, was a miscellany of tribal villages, each settled on one of the many hills grouped round the Citadel; or so
it is assumed from the plural form of the names of the principal
cities (Mykenai, Thebai, Athenai). Each village appears to
have been a separate unit with its own burial ground near by.
In the neighbourhood of the Citadel were imposing buildings
concerned with the business of the king or, as some claim, the
houses of the great merchants. Three of these houses lie in a
Plate 40   row just by the modern road and distant about 150 yards from
Fig. 36   the acropolis. According to their principal finds they have
been named (from north to south) the House of Shields, The
House of the Oil Merchant, and the House of Sphinxes. The

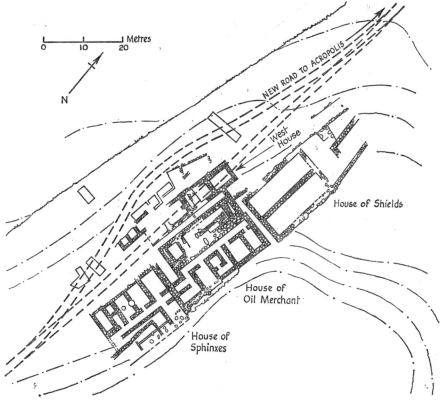

Fig. 36. *Houses outside the Citadel, Mycenae (after Chadwick)*

northernmost house is much ruined and only the plan of two
great rooms side by side with entrances apparently at the north
can be made out. The second house is built on an artificial
terrace held up by a massive retaining wall. The western half is
at a higher level and represents the main storey of the building,
but only the plan of the basement to the east is well preserved.
It has a long corridor running almost the whole length of the
house, off which open various store-rooms. One of these contained large pithoi, or storage jars, that were almost certainly
used for olive oil – a tablet with a record of this commodity was
found in this room. Because of their great size they had to be

supported on two sides by low walls of crude brick. Further‑
more, the floor was raised near the entrance to prevent the es‑
cape of spilt oil. The third house, that of the Sphinxes, also
consists of a basement only and the arrangement of store‑rooms
off a long corridor is very similar. From the ruins of this house
(and others in the Citadel) it is possible to calculate the height
Fig. 36 of the basement at about 1.50 m. (5 feet). The West House,
recently revealed when the modern road was shifted further to
the west, immediately adjoins the above‑mentioned houses but
does not appear to be connected with them. Owing to its
ruined state its plan cannot be made out with certainty, but it
seems to have included a building with megaron, vestibule,
and porch.

The plan of a house, other than that of the basement area, has
in fact seldom been preserved, but where this has happened it is
Fig. 31 often found to be of the megaron form. A house at Korakou,
near Corinth, has such a plan. It has a built porch preceding
the vestibule, and the living room (megaron) had a column on
either side of a central hearth, which was made up of coarse
Fig. 35 potsherds set in clay. Within the Citadel of Mycenae several
houses have been excavated of which the best known are the
Granary by the Lion Gate and the so‑called House of the
Warrior Vase near the Grave Circle; but they have been so
thoroughly looted that it is no longer possible to determine their
purpose, with the possible exception of the Granary. The so‑
called Citadel House, which includes part of the South House
and perhaps part of Tsountas's House, seems to have been an
administration building from its size and the fact that many of
its rooms are in self‑contained units. It is, however, only partly
excavated. A novel feature in this house was a sloping corridor
or ramp, one wall of which was decorated with a stone dado.
Fig. 37 One house, known as the House of Columns, seems to have
been a Mycenaean palace in miniature. Though it is much
ruined and the plan is difficult to reconstruct, it is clear that it

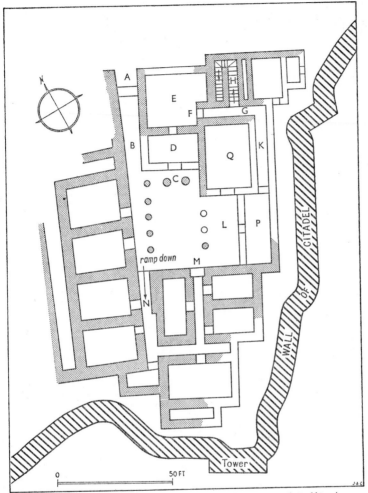

Fig. 37. Plan of the House of Columns, Mycenae (after Wace and Stubbings)

had a colonnaded court, which gave access to a megaron-type
of building and at a lower level to store-rooms.

The form of Mycenaean houses was often determined by the
lie of the land. Normally high ground or rocky hill – and the

103

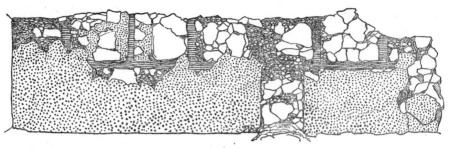

Fig. 38 Plastered and timbered walls. South House, Mycenae (after Wace)

▬▬▬ Grooves in masonry showing position of wooden tie-beams
▦▦▦ Outer coat of plaster
▩▩▩ Clay and pebble backing for plaster

0 _____ 1 metre

Fig. 38

rock is never far from the surface in Greece – was chosen for settlement. A house with any depth and built on the side of a hill had two storeys and perhaps three. The lower one, the basement, would have the rock as a floor, which was either sloping and uneven or partly levelled. The walls of basements were solidly built of rubble, the thickness varying with the size and weight of the superstructure that had to be held up. The wall was often built with a framework of wood, a form of reinforcement, or so it is believed, against earthquakes. This consisted of upright posts placed at equal intervals on both faces of the wall and tied to one another by crosspieces passing through the thickness of the wall. There were also horizontal beams let into the faces of the wall at various levels. The form of construction, however, was not uniform in every building. The 'half-timbering' was seldom, if ever, visible. In basement rooms it was concealed by a coating of mud-plaster, in living or public rooms by decoration of superior quality. In the latter case the surface was usually made of a fine stucco that was frequently painted with frescoes.

The storey above the basement is almost invariably of mud-brick construction. Three different styles of this work have been recognized at Mycenae: walls built entirely of sun-dried bricks, walls built of hard-packed clay or mud, and a combination of brick and hard-packed clay. In the first instance bricks with varying dimensions, of which the largest were approximately 60 × 40 × 10 cms (24 × 16 × 4 inches), were used. The length of the brick (60 cm.) corresponds as a rule to the thickness of the wall. The second type of wall construction may have been produced in the same way as concrete, that is, within a wooden mould. The third type has a core of clay, reinforced with rubble, and facings of mud-brick. A modified version of half-timbering was also used in combination with mud-brick walls.

There is much discussion concerning the form of the roof. That of the later Greek temple was gabled, but few roof tiles belonging to Mycenaean buildings have ever been found, and so it is likely that the roof was flat as are those of so many Greek houses today. This statement finds some support from a fresco fragment portraying a warrior falling from a flat-roofed building. Fragments of burnt roofing, with impressions in clay of brushwood and beam, show that the same technique was used as in modern village houses, namely, brushwood or wattle laid across joists and covered with a coating of mud-plaster and hard-packed earth. Such a construction could serve as the floor of an upper storey if this existed. The floors in the poorer houses, as today in Greece, were of stamped earth, but in the more well-to-do dwellings they had a covering of white plaster.

Fig. 39

As the ruins of a Mycenaean building are so often reduced to the bare foundations, it is very rarely that one finds evidence for windows. Two were identified in the Granary at Mycenae, where the walls are preserved to a height of about 6 feet. The doorway was often treated with special care, at least in palaces and larger residences. The door-jamb was built in many cases of rubble and mudbrick, sheathed with wood. The threshold was either of wood or of stone. In the great reception rooms of

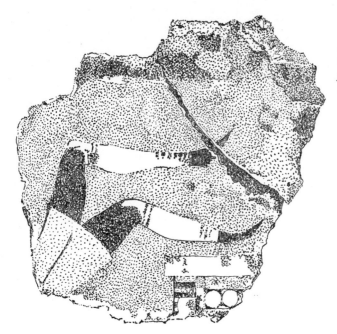

Fig. 39. Warrior fall-ing from a roof. Fresco fragment, Mycenae (after Bossert)

the palace at Mycenae and in the so-called House of Columns near by, the thresholds are enormous blocks of conglomerate. A lot of work has gone into the finish of this very tough stone. The upper surface has been smoothed by careful dressing to a fine polish except for shallow emplacements for the door-jambs that are sharply cut out at either side, The grooves left by the bronze saw which was used to cut these emplacements and the ledge that acted as the doorstop are often visible. In one corner of the threshold – or in two, if there were double doors – a hemispherical socket was hollowed out in which the doorpost could revolve. Sometimes traces of bronze have been found in these sockets. It is possible that in the palaces the threshold and the wood-work of the doors were sheathed in bronze. (In gate-ways such as the Lion Gate at Mycenae and the Great Gate at Tiryns the sockets for the timbers that barred the doors are still to be seen.)

Staircases in houses were normally constructed of wood which has naturally perished. In some buildings, such as the Granary and the House of Columns at Mycenae, their exist-ence can be inferred with a fair degree of certainty from the remains of rubble piers in the centre of the presumed stair well. The basements of some houses had no doors and could only be entered from above by a ladder. Such houses would very often, it is presumed, have an outside wooden staircase, as in Greek villages today.

Fig. 37

The problem of the water supply was a serious one in sum-mer, just as it is today. It was of particular importance during a siege. Several ingenious systems were devised to overcome the difficulty. At Mycenae a secret cistern (sometimes wrongly referred to as the Perseia Fountain) was constructed at the end

Figs. 35: S,
40

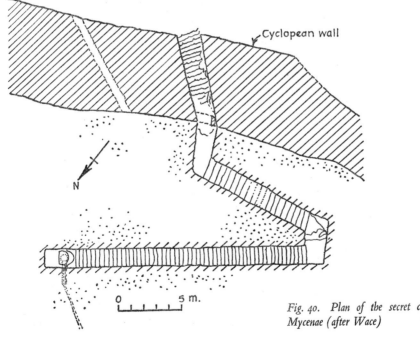

Cyclopean wall

N

0   5 m.

Fig. 40. Plan of the secret cistern, Mycenae (after Wace)

Plate 42

of the thirteenth century, which is a marvel of engineering. Three flights of steps lead down to the reservoir. The first flight is built within the fortification walls. The other two are con/ structed underground and outside the walls. The cistern was fed from the spring called Perseia (after the hero Perseus), which flows to this day and is situated about 200 yards from the Ci/ tadel on higher ground. It is presumed that the water was brought by an underground channel but no evidence for this has ever been found except for some terracotta pipes leading into the opening in the roof above the cistern. The cistern itself is not of great size, but the capacity was enormously increased when the water was allowed to flood the whole of the lower flight of steps where the rock vault rises to a height of over 12 feet; and to prevent seepage this part of the staircase was covered with waterproof cement, which is still preserved. Neither the location nor even the existence of this reservoir could be known to the enemy except through treachery. Once known, the Cita/ del was doomed.

At Athens the system was more secure, as an artificial well on the north slopes of the acropolis was within the defences. A shaft of great depth was sunk in a natural cleft of the rock, which allowed sufficient room for a stairway of seven flights to give access to the well. The first two flights were of wood, the remaining five of stone, which was partly supported by rubble masonry and partly anchored to the sheer face of the rock by means of wooden cross ties.

It has always been a mystery how Pylos was able to cope with the water problem in time of siege, and indeed with defence in general. Although the sides of the hill on which the palace buildings are situated are, or had been made, precipitous, the advantages of the site as a natural fortress cannot compare with those of other Mycenaean sites, nor were its deficiencies in this respect made good by powerful fortification walls. Of Cyclo/ pean walls there is no trace. However, where there is no security

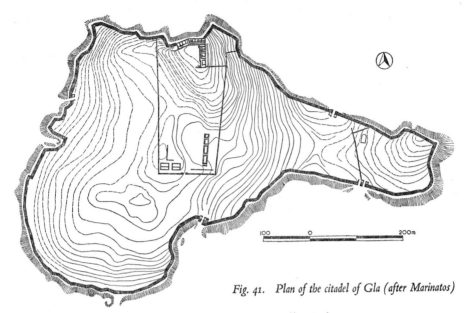

Fig. 41. Plan of the citadel of Gla (after Marinatos)

of water supply, of what use are the strongest walls? Pylos must have depended on her strong right arm to defend herself.

Pylos was not the only Mycenaean city with limited natural means of defence. Little is known about Thebes as so much of the ancient city lies beneath the modern town and cannot therefore be excavated, but it does not appear to have had any impressive fortification walls, nor is the site naturally a very strong one. Ancient Iolkos, renowned in legend as the city from which the Argonauts set sail, overshadowed by Mount Pelion from whose forests the timber for the Argo was hewn, is now enveloped in the modern town of Volos. Its site has only recently been recognised and very little excavation has taken place. But this illustrious city, though set on a hill, does not appear to have had formidable means of defence.

The great Mycenaean fortresses whose majestic ruined walls can still be seen are Mycenae, Tiryns, Midea, Asine, and Gla on the mainland, and Phylakopi on the island of Melos. Little is known concerning Gla in Boeotia. In Classical times it was

Plates 35, 43

Fig. 41

109

an island in a great lake, the former Lake Copais. It now stands as a low, rocky hummock in a sea of rice and cotton fields, for the lake has been drained in modern times. However, a great dyke, believed to be Mycenaean, suggests that the lake was also drained in the Mycenaean period. All that remains today of Gla is the skeletal plan of the palace and the magnificent, partly demolished fortification walls, 15 feet thick, that follow the contours of the 'island'. (The scheme of the palace is completely individual. There is no central court dominated by the megaron and its antechambers. Instead, the buildings, with no room of any great size, are laid out in the shape of an L. It is possible that the plan was conditioned by the terrain and considerations of defence.) The walls of Midea, not far distant from Mycenae, are still extant and they are comparatively well preserved. But it is at Tiryns and Mycenae that these awe-inspiring walls, now largely restored but impressive formerly even in their ruin, can be seen as once they appeared to would-be invaders who must have gazed on them with amazement not unmixed with fear.

To the later Greeks the building of these walls appeared to be beyond the powers of man. Only a race of giants, the one-eyed Cyclopes, could have raised such stones, and Cyclopean is the name that has been used for these walls and all like constructions ever since. In Egypt there was a long tradition of handling blocks of even greater size. One system used there was the construction of a great ramp of earth up which the large blocks were hauled to the required height and then placed in position. As the building rose, so the ramp was raised and lengthened, so that the gradient might not become too steep. There is no reason why this simple but laborious system should not have been used for the building of Cyclopean walls; but of course we do not know. A similar theory has been advanced for the raising and placing in position of the enormous lintels over the doorways of the tholos tombs (the inner lintel of the

Plate 43

Plate 44

Treasury of Atreus is estimated to weigh 120 tons). In such Plate 23
cases the side of the hill would correspond to a ramp.

The large boulders used in Cyclopean walls were only partly
hammer-dressed and many not at all. The foundation layer was
set on a packing of small stones. Other courses were laid on dry
and any gaps were filled with clay and small stones. In fortification walls the thickness averaged about 15 feet; at Mycenae this
is sometimes as much as 22 feet. Cyclopean blocks, however,
are only used for the faces of the wall; the core is rubble and
earth. Another style in building, conspicuous at Mycenae and
Pylos, was ashlar masonry. Large symmetrical blocks were
dressed by hammer and cut by saw. The courses are more re-
gular and evenly laid than in Cyclopean building. This style
can be seen in the walls and bastion to either side of the Lion Plates 15, 44
Gate; it adds great dignity to the approach. It was also used in
some of the tholoi, particularly the late ones at Mycenae. The
most impressive examples are the Treasury of Atreus and the Plate 22
'Tomb of Clytemnestra'.

Used in conjunction with both Cyclopean and ashlar masonry is corbelling. This system had long been familiar to
countries in the Near East and was used in the making of a
false arch or vault. To create the curve each course of masonry
is made to project beyond, or overhang, the one below. In the
case of an arch the projecting courses of the opposite piers
finally meet. The underside of the overhanging stones can then
be carved away to form a semicircle or false arch. In Mycenaean architecture a pointed arch was preferred, and this might
involve the use of but two courses and sometimes only one,
particularly if Cyclopean blocks were being used. This style of
architecture is well exemplified by the roofs of the famous galleries at Tiryns and of their adjacent storage chambers, all Cyclo- Plate 46
pean-built. Such constructions by being incorporated in the
thickness of the walls saved valuable space, or rather created it
for much needed purposes. At the same time the 'Gothic win-

Plate 42

Fig. 35: T

dows' in the storage chambers provided embrasures from which an attacking force could be harassed. Corbel construction is often found in the Mycenae acropolis. The roof of the stairway to the secret cistern is built in that fashion; and near by there is the Sally Port, a tunnel with a pointed roof passing right through the walls that are 22 feet thick at that point. The main drains in the Citadel, which debouch through the walls, are built in the same manner. But the examples that are most familiar to the visitor are the relieving triangle above the Lion Gate and those above the great portals of the late tholos tombs. Roman architects adopted the same principle, creating arches over weak points in the structure of a building to deflect the stress from the superstructure on to the stronger piers. The weakest point in the doorway was the lintel block and the Mycenaeans had learnt from experience that this was the first to give way under stress – nearly all the lintels in the early tholoi have crashed. But the triangular space as now seen in the Treasury of Atreus, for instance, would not have been visible in the finished monument. It was filled by a panel of the same shape, of which the only surviving but magnificent witness is the tympanum relief over the Lion Gate.

Fig. 42

The history of the tholos tombs has been described elsewhere (see p. 79). It now remains to say something about their construction. The earliest one known (excepting perhaps the one in Thessaly) is in Messenia. Exceptionally, it was constructed underground; that is, a circular shaft to contain the monument was sunk in level ground instead of in the side of a hill, which is the more normal practice. Another anomaly is the construction of a tholos above ground. This occurs in parts of Messenia and in Euboea. The tholoi there were covered with a mound after completion. This method was not adopted elsewhere as apparently it was realized that the mound provided insufficient pressure on the upper part of the tomb to counteract the outward thrust of the vault, which consequently collapsed in most

Fig. 42. Reconstruction of the façade of the Treasury of Atreus (after Wace)

113

cases. Greater pressure was provided in the majority of tombs by the sides of the hill in which they were built.

In constructing the earlier tombs very small, undressed stones were used. They were selected for their flatness. The thickness of the wall in the smaller tombs may be not more than 3 feet. The lower part of the wall was normally built vertically, like a drum, up to about one quarter of the height planned for the tomb. Thereafter the diameter of the tomb gradually contracts as each succeeding course overlaps the one below, corbel-wise, and thus the vault is formed. The topmost course is a single

Fig. 43

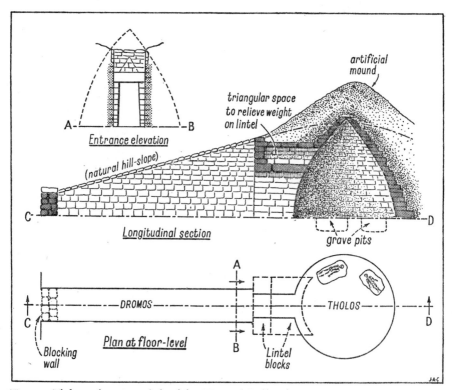

Fig. 43. Tholos tomb, section and plan (after Wace and Stubbings)

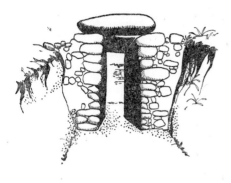

EPANO PHOURNOS

KATO PHOURNOS

CLYTEMNESTRA

Fig. 44. Evolution of the doorway and dromos of tholoi at Mycenae (after Helen Wace)

capping-stone. The space between the outer vault and the circular shaft in which the tomb was built was then tightly packed with earth and a mound raised over the point of the dome. With advances in building technique ever larger stones were used, and these were carefully shaped on the under surface to produce the curve of the vault. In the final development enormous blocks were used, and perfection was attained in the dome of the Treasury of Atreus. (Exceptionally, this tomb and the tholos at Orchomenos, described by Pausanias as the 'Treasury of Minyas', have a side-chamber which was not vaulted. It is rock-cut at Mycenae, stone-built at Orchomenos.)

Two other components enter into the construction of a tholos tomb: the doorway and the dromos. Each shows devel-opment over the centuries and this is best demonstrated by the evolution traceable in the nine tholoi of Mycenae, although it does not follow that this evolution is valid for other parts of Greece. The lintels of the doorways associated with the earliest tombs, those built with very small slabs, are short and have no relieving triangles. Large blocks are used for the door jambs but the construction is not always equal to the stresses put upon them. Thresholds are not found. In later tholoi structural im-provements can be noted. The lintel is longer and often survives through the relief of pressure afforded by the empty triangular space above it, and the door jambs are built of solid ashlar masonry. Thresholds of sawn conglomerate are introduced. The one in the Treasury of Atreus is a model of exact fitting. As it was impossible to obtain a close-fitting of the threshold if made in one block, two pieces were used. Wedges of poros limestone were then inserted between the two conglomerate blocks and driven home to press them securely against the door jambs. The evolution of the dromos or passage-way leading up to the tomb can be briefly described. At first, the corridor is cut in the rock and unlined by masonry. When it was found that the sides of the dromos often collapsed, later examples were lined with rubble. The final stage is to be seen in the magnifi-cent approaches to the later tholos tombs, when ashlar conglom-erate was used.

At an early period the importance of keeping moisture out of the tomb was realised, for the seepage of water into the joints very quickly undermined the structure. To counteract this danger at Mycenae, layers of *plesia*, a waterproof clay extant in the district, were alternated with earth in covering the dome. Three such layers were used for the protection of the vault of the

Fig. 44

Fig. 45

Plate 30

Plate 22

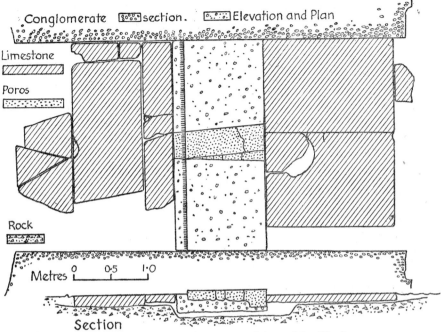

Conglomerate. Section. Elevation and Plan

Limestone

Poros

Rock

Metres 0 0·5 1·0

Section

Fig. 45. Plan and section of the threshold of the Treasury of Atreus (after Wace)

so-called 'Tomb of Aegisthus' (fifteenth century); even so the vault collapsed. The latest tholos at Mycenae is the 'Tomb of Clytemnestra' of the thirteenth century. Many centuries of architectural knowledge are incorporated in this monument. And in 1952/3 a new feature was revealed. At that time Professor Wace uncovered a curving wall of very handsome appearance that formed an arc to the east of the 'Tomb of Clytemnestra'. This was the retaining wall, built of poros, which served to support the mound over the tholos. (Traces of a similar retaining wall have been found for the Treasury of Atreus.) Furthermore, there is evidence that a white coating of plaster had been used for the top layer of this mound, an unusual and striking form of embellishment. This tomb, therefore, may have

Fig. 29

117

been the one that Pausanias (see p. 15) describes as the tomb of Atreus, head of the house of Atreidae and father of Agamemnon. (He was already familiar with the earlier tomb which, because it was open, he described as a treasury.) Alternately, as only relative and not absolute dates can be given for these tholoi, the 'Tomb of Clytemnestra' could be that of Agamemnon and the earlier tholos that of Atreus, with whose name it is traditionally associated. But these are speculations that probably never will be confirmed.

CHAPTER V

Daily Life and the Arts

IN DISCUSSING THE DWELLINGS of the mighty and the less exalted, descriptions have largely been confined to the buildings, and little has been said about those who lived in them. It is very seldom that articles directly concerned with the more personal side of daily life are found in context. Such objects as survive *in situ* are crockery, storage vessels, and so on, which had little interest for the despoilers; for the majority of the palaces and houses that have been under review were destroyed by fire and this, it seems, followed on the systematic looting of everything of worth on the premises. Naturally some articles of value were overlooked and others cast aside because they were damaged. It is only by these that the archaeologist is provided with some clue concerning the use of the building, though seldom of the room. For almost invariably the more personal objects have fallen from an upper storey and do not belong to the rooms in which they have been found. In houses it is usually only the basement that survives, and in palaces the public rooms. Our knowledge of the daily life of the Mycenaeans has therefore to be gleaned from very indirect sources: frescoes, scenes depicted on vases, metalwork, ivories, and more recently, the tablets.

We know next to nothing of the movable furniture of the houses from archaeological finds. One type of 'fixture' that has survived on the spot, however, is the plastered bench. This is quite a prominent feature in the palaces and to a lesser extent in the richer houses. Such benches are often found in what may be interpreted as waiting-rooms; certainly where bureaucracies are concerned, they would be an essential piece of furniture. It is quite a common scene today to see Greeks seated on a bench, patiently waiting their turn at a bank or government office. But

FURNITURE

benches seem also to have been used as shelves, or as a support for free-standing shelving as appears to have been the case in the archives room at Pylos. The existence of beds and chairs had been presumed from the knowledge that such furniture was in use in Minoan Crete, but the decisive evidence for these was recently supplied by the tablets. An extract from one of the furniture tablets reads as follows: 'One ebony(?) footstool inlaid with figures of men and lions in ivory... One footstool inlaid with a man and a horse and an octopus and a palm-tree(?) in ivory.' Two striking facts emerge from these inventories: that

Fig. 23

the footstool was a frequent piece of furniture in the palace, and that it was expensively embellished. The description in the inventory of the inlay decoration may require us to revise our ideas about the many fragments of burnt ivories found in excavations (the fact of their burning has preserved them for posterity). It is usually assumed that they formed part of the inlay of caskets, and no doubt they often did. There is a wooden box from Shaft Grave V which is decorated with ivory animal figures; another example is the casket borne by the lady in the Tiryns fresco. But many of the ivories found in the House of

Plate 45

Shields and in the House of Sphinxes in Mycenae could as well have decorated furniture as caskets. The various elements

Fig. 46

such as rosette, ivy leaf, lily, murex shell, dolphin – all motives incidentally that occur on the pottery – would be well suited to either purpose, but the miniature columns, of which such a great diversity was found in the House of Sphinxes would perhaps be more in place in a larger frame, such as a footstool. Tables, according to the tablets, could be of stone, ivory, or ebony, and they are described as being inlaid with cyanus (paste), gold, and ivory.

The quality, variety and comparative abundance of the furniture described in the tablets could not have been inferred from the results of excavation hitherto. The wealth of the shaft graves and other occasional rich finds have been considered as

Fig. 46. Ivory inlays. Rosette, ivy leaf, lily, murex shell, and dolphin (after Bennett)

isolated examples. Our ideas have now to be revised. Sufficient allowance has not been made for the enormous gaps in our knowledge created by the plunderer. Other furnishings that are not mentioned in the tablets can only be surmised. The Mycenaeans were well versed in the arts of weaving. Upholstery of some kind would not be beyond their powers, and rugs and skins are found in both primitive and civilized communities.

The fashions of dress, at least for the women, were originally   DRESS dictated by Minoan society and it is surprising to find that there should have been no noticeable change throughout the whole of the Mycenaean age. The dress worn by the goddess from Shaft Grave III (sixteenth century) is not recognizably different from that of the woman portrayed on the ivory handle from the 'Tomb of Clytemnestra' (thirteenth century) or from any other representation of the same period such as the ivory group from Mycenae. The latter is perhaps the best example as it shows the   Plates 12, 13 dress in great detail, the bare bosoms, the tight bodice with short sleeves, and the flounced and pleated skirt of many complications. The shawl, shared by both ladies, was of particularly fine workmanship and was bordered with a fringe of tassels. One of the ladies wears her hair down her back, carefully waved and ending in a point. Her companion has a different coiffure; the hair is tightly fitted to the shape of the head, but one tress has been carried across the top to make a kind of bandeau. If, as has been suggested, mother and daughter are to be recognized in this group, the simpler hair style may represent the younger generation.

Plate 47

Costumes of women of the ruling class were frequently adorned with gold sequins or rosettes, and the hems of the jackets bordered with thin gold plate; so it appears from the frescoes. Pieces of gold foil of these shapes have been found in tombs and are usually perforated with one or more holes for sewing on to the dress. The jewellery worn by the women in the ivory group described above can be matched by examples found in chamber tombs. At that period the beads were usual-

Plates 48, 49

ly of gold or of coloured opaque glass, but in an earlier age they could be of amethyst, carnelian, amber and gold. Ropes of beads were often worn, the number of ropes being controlled

Figs. 64, 66

by spacer-beads, which would allow from two to four 'gar-lands'. Heavy and elaborate gold ear-rings were the fashion

Plate 50

during the Shaft Grave period, but in the fourteenth/thirteenth centuries a gold rosette or a simple penannular ring was pre-ferred. Very gorgeous trappings were found in the shaft graves,

Plate 27
Plate 51

huge – and it must be admitted vulgar – gold 'tiaras' adorn-ing the women, gold pectorals and armlets the men; but it is doubtful whether these were worn in real life. They must have been intended for burial only, in accord with the rich and sumptuous examples of Egyptian custom.

Plate 53

The work-a-day dress for men, at least in warm weather, was a loin cloth or short kilt; there are many such representations in Mycenaean art. The formal dress as pictured in frescoes was a

Plate 54
Fig. 39

simple tunic with short sleeves, a narrow waist, and a rather full but short 'skirt'. Very often leggings were worn. Anyone who has had to make his way through the thick and thorny scrub of Greece would appreciate the advantages of this protection. The

Plate 38

bard in the fresco from the throne-room at Pylos wears a close-fitting costume that reaches down to the ankles. The lower part of it is pleated and perhaps flounced, as different colours are shown in bands. The upper part of the dress is doubled in some fashion to form a kind of short cape. The man's hair is long and one curl falls in front of the ear in the Minoan fashion. The

Fig. 47.   Buttons or whorls (after Furumark)

dress and hair style are altogether unusual and uncharacteristic; they suggest priestly attire. Men often wore beards, but the upper lip was usually shaven. The hair was not allowed, as a rule, to fall below the shoulders. A frequent find in tombs is a trun⁄ cated cone, pierced axially, made of terracotta in LH I and II and of steatite in LH III. It is like a spindle⁄whorl in shape, but such large numbers of them have been found associated with single burials, that they are generally interpreted as buttons. The gilded bone plaques incised with intricate designs from the shaft graves are thought to be buttons. They are unique and must be regarded as part of the paraphernalia of burial.

Signet rings were worn by both men and women in high posi⁄ tion. They were either of gold or silver, rarely of bronze. Gold can weather time, but silver oxidizes. Consequently few exam⁄ ples of the latter survive. The oval⁄shaped bezel, normally at right angles to the hoop and therefore in line with the finger, was engraved with skill and with a fine feeling for composition. The craft was learnt from the Minoans. Closely related to the signet ring and its precursor in time is the engraved seal⁄stone or gem, which had a long history in Crete. The earliest My⁄ cenaean gems, those of the Shaft Grave period, are very likely of Minoan workmanship. The seals were made in a variety of

Plate 52

Fig. 47

ORNAMENTS
AND GEMS

Plates 8, 10

Plate 55

shapes, circular and lentoid, oval, oblong, and amygdaloid (almond-shaped). In the early Mycenaean period they were of hard stones, such as amethyst, carnelian, sard, haematite, etc. In LH III the softer steatite (or soapstone) was generally pre-ferred. The instruments used were a fine drill and graver. The themes were both secular and religious. Oriental influence is to be discerned in the antithetical composition of some of the sub-jects. Apart from their talismanic properties, the principal use of gem and signet ring known to us is for the sealing of stores. A lump of clay was affixed with string to the mouth of a storage jar or any other object that had to be sealed. While the clay was still soft it was impressed with the seal and usually a Linear B inscription was added. Thus the object was labelled as well as receiving a proprietary mark. Clay sealings have been

Fig. 48

found at Mycenae, Pylos, and at the Menelaion near Sparta. They are usually prism-shaped and often show the impression of string marks and finger-prints. Seal-stones are found with burials, sometimes in great numbers. From their position in relation to the skeleton they appear to have been worn on a string round the wrist. There are many fine examples of the engraver's

Plate 55

art, but quite outstanding is the Griffin seal found in a tholos tomb near the palace at Pylos. The griffins standing guard over the throne of Nestor have already been described, but the oblong gold seal, on which the royal griffin is portrayed with such finesse and majesty, belongs to an earlier period, LH II (or late fifteenth century).

FOOD

The normal diet cannot have been very different from what it is today. The basic ingredients remain the same. For meat there was principally mutton or lamb, goat, pork, and beef. The tablets at Knossos record great quantities of sheep, and the Grecian countryside is equally well suited for the grazing of sheep and goats. Cattle, then as now, were more rare. Pig bones have been identified and, apart from the meat of domesticated animals, there were the rewards of the chase: venison, wild

boar, hares, duck, geese and partridge. Hunting wild game was
a favourite activity of the Mycenaeans and is frequently portrayed in their art. Among the more dangerous pursuits was the
lion hunt. The stela from Shaft Grave V shows a huntsman in
a chariot in full gallop after the prey. At other times the combat
was on foot, as is vividly pictured on one of the inlaid daggers   Plate 56
from Shaft Grave IV. There several men attack a pride of lions
with bow and spear. In other scenes engraved on gems the
battle is more even; a warrior takes on a lion single-handed and
does not always come out best from the fray. The tablets record
that hounds were used in the chase and a krater fragment from
Messenia shows one of them in pursuit of a stag. A scene (ad-
mittedly Egyptian-inspired) on a dagger blade from Shaft
Grave V suggests that cats were trained to stalk wild duck, as in
a later age hawks would be used in falconry. Though Homer
rarely mentions the eating of fish, fish-bones have been found at
Mycenae and Thebes, and cockleshells occur in abundance. It
can be assumed therefore that the protein diet was heavily supplemented from the sea, for few countries can boast of a longer
coast-line than Greece and the fish of the Mediterranean are
renowned for their savour. Shellfish of all kinds were popular.
The murex and the octopus are favourite subjecs on vases, and   Figs. 15, 24
the latter was no doubt considered a delicacy as it is today. But
the staple diet would have been bread made from wheat or
barley. According to the tablets, the flour was ground by the
women and baked by the men. From the same source we learn
of the production of cheese. It would be derived presumably, as
today, from sheep and goats. Vegetables such as peas, beans,
vetches, and lentils are known from excavations. Fruits and

nuts are less well documented, but the usual Mediterranean varieties such as figs, pears, apples, pomegranates (shown on gems), almonds, walnuts and hazelnuts are to be expected; the plum tree is native to Greece. Two important natural products mentioned in the tablets are wine and honey. Olive oil, for which there is both archaeological and written evidence – the latter recording large quantities – must have been one of the most important sources of wealth. It could be used for cooking and lighting and there was perhaps a surplus available for export.

COOKING UTENSILS From the above resources an accomplished cook could produce a variety of appetizing meals aided by all manner of spices, such as those recorded on the tablets from the House of Sphinxes. For the preparation of meals and the manner of their serving we have to rely on Homeric descriptions, but as the art of cooking is conservative by nature, his account no doubt holds true for Mycenaean times. Fragments of cooking pots are one of the commonest finds on Mycenaean settlements. Bronze cauldrons figure in the tablets and several specimens have been found, mostly in tombs. Other varieties of bronze vessels used in the kitchen or at table were jugs and amphorae for wine and water, but these would only be found in the houses of the well-to-do. The poorer classes would have to rely upon clay substitutes. For that reason many clay vessels show the influence of metallic models and are often copied from them. This is very noticeable in the case of the so-called Vapheio cup (see p. 49), of which there are many fine examples in gold and silver from the shaft graves.

Plate 24

Plate 57

GOLD AND SILVER ARTICLES The wealth of the shaft graves in precious vessels – and it is noticeable that they far exceed in number those made of clay from the same tombs – gives some idea of the display of 'gold and silver plate' that could be laid out at a royal feast. Even the richest families could not hope to vie with such affluence, but in fourteenth-century Midea (Dendra) about 150 years later

(LH III A) the sovereign of that principality was laid to rest in his vaulted tomb with no mean treasure, not comparable, it is true, in quantity with that of the shaft graves but certainly in quality and artistic merit.

Plate 58

These instances are from the very few unplundered tombs in Mycenaean Greece. By good fortune a grave pit in the tholos near Vapheio (see p. 49) was overlooked by the robbers who stripped the tomb. In it were found the two famous cups, exquisite works of Minoan craftmanship, or so it is believed by many; but the date of the tomb is LH II, a period when the Mycenaeans, having served close upon two centuries of tutorship under Minoan artists, were producing work of high quality in their own right. On these cups are portrayed with great delicacy and feeling various scenes connected with the cycle of bull-leaping, a dangerous sport that may have had a religious significance. The tale is told in consecutive scenes that follow one another round the two cups. In the first scene the bull is attracted by a decoy cow. His attention thus engaged, he is caught unawares by the trainer and tethered by the foot. On the second cup the bull is seen struggling in a net; he is in captivity. But later on he is seen venting his rage on two athletes, both of whom are in dire peril, if not doomed. This same sport was vividly illustrated in a thirteenth-century fresco from the palace at Tiryns. The game or ritual had had a long tradition in Crete, where it may have formed the foundation for the legend of Theseus and the Minotaur.

Plate 4

Plate 3

Silver figures quite prominently in the shaft grave treasures. Outstanding is a silver funnel-shaped rhyton, or filler, from Tomb IV. It is decorated in repoussé with scenes of battle and of a city undergoing siege. Unfortunately, but few fragments of this unique vessel have survived. Two other magnificent rhytons from this same tomb are in the form of an animal's head. The liquid issued from the mouth and it is likely that these vessels were used ritually for libations. One, shaped as a lion's

Plate 59

Plate 17

head is of gold; the other, in the form of a bull's head, is of gold and silver. These two metals were also used, with niello (a black amalgam) for the very critical and delicate inlay work on metal. Superb examples of this technique are to be seen in the

Plates 28, 56   inlaid daggers from the shaft graves, and from the tholos of Routsi (LH II). A silver cup from Dendra (LH III A) is decorated with bulls' heads in a similar technique.

STONE   Not many examples of craftsmanship in stone survive and the
CARVING   sculpture of figures in the round does not appear to have been
Plate 20   attempted on a large scale. The shaft grave stelae (see p. 74) exhibit the earliest efforts at stone carving. The work is crude and the artist was not fully master of his material. He is most successful in the execution of the spiral borders, but when it comes to representing the figures they are treated in a similar manner, that is, they are merely blocked out and no attempt is made at modelling. A strong sense of movement, however, is introduced. After this early period no major works in stone carving are found until the thirteenth century. The outstanding

Plate 15   example is, of course, the relief of lions (or rather lionesses) over the Lion Gate. The heads are missing, but it is clear that they were sculptured separately as there is a dowel hole in the neck of each beast to secure them. They were probably made in some other stone, perhaps steatite which is a lighter material. There are differing interpretations as to the symbolism of this famous relief, some emphasizing the religious aspects, others the secular; but all are agreed in recognizing in this early example of Greek sculpture a great monument, noble and majestic in conception, and a worthy precursor of later Greek genius.

There must have been several such sculptured reliefs, the purpose of which would have been to conceal the triangular relieving-space above the lintel (see p. 112). Parts of the sculptured façade of the Treasury of Atreus have been preserved and several reconstructions of its original form have been attempted. Most of the elements are sculptured spirals, but there are two tantalizing fragments in low relief, found near the tomb, that formed part of a bull-leaping scene. Their style strongly recalls that of the Vapheio gold cups. Among the sculptured fragments from this same tomb are architectural elements with a 'trig-lyph' pattern, so called from its resemblance to the similar de-coration on the entablature of Doric temples. In the Mycenaean version there are three vertical fillets (the 'triglyph') flanked on either side by half-rosettes, which are carved in fairly high relief. This pattern repeated was a popular form of architectural de-coration and frequently used in the adornment of the palaces, though indeed very few pieces have survived. When found *in situ* it is at the base of a wall or bench, and it is in that position that it is usually portrayed in frescoes.

Figs. 23, 42
Plate 55

Fig. 34

The implements employed in stone carving were the tubular drill, the saw, and the chisel. A fast-revolving reed, supple-mented by sand and water, was probably used for drilling the holes. Sand and water also would be necessary to assist the work of the bronze saw which was slightly toothed or plain. The chisel, also of bronze, was used for the finishing touches and some kind of polishing process with abrasives would fol-low. The mark of the drill is clearly to be seen in the fashioning of stone vases. The inside of the vessel, particularly if it had a rather narrow mouth, could only be hollowed out in this man-ner; and as the external appearance of the vase was alone im-portant, the inside is often left unfinished with the stumps of broken-off cylindrical cores showing. A large number of stone vases were found in the House of Shields at Mycenae. They were of serpentine, limestone, pudding-stone and *lapis Lacedae-monius*, a dark green mottled stone from an area to the south of Sparta. An admirable example of fine workmanship in this hard stone is the fluted rhyton, unfortunately incomplete, found on the acropolis of Mycenae. The surface of these stone vases was sometimes carved to receive ornamental inlays of paste or semi-precious stones.

Plate 60

SCULPTURE IN THE ROUND

Plate 19

Plate 53

Plates 12, 13

Although it is difficult to generalize because of the scanty sur, viving material, it seems that sculpture in the round was largely confined to small figures, and these are mainly of terracotta. Of exceptional size in terracotta are the cult statues from Keos and the stuccoed head from Mycenae (see p. 70), but as a rule the figures are seldom more than 5 in. high. A unique example in lead is a statuette of a youth from a grave near Kampos, Laco, nia. And then there is the remarkable ivory group from My, cenae (see p. 121). It is a masterpiece and represents a field in which the Mycenaean artist excelled.

IVORY RELIEFS

Plates 45, 61, 62, 64

Plate 45

Fig. 49

But ivory figures in the round are rare. The greater part of the work that has survived is in relief, such as the carving on ivory combs, on the handles of mirrors, on pyxides (boxes), and the ivory panels made for the adornment of caskets, as well as the inlays for furniture and even for chariots – according to the tab, lets. The early period (LH I and II) is not so well documen, ted; examples are chiefly from the shaft graves and from tholos tombs in Messenia. However, at that time, when the influence, if not the hand, of the Minoan artist is so apparent, the work cannot be taken as truly representative of Mycenaean achieve, ment. As in other domains of art, LH III was the great period in which the Mycenaean genius fulfilled itself. By that time it had absorbed what Crete had to offer and felt sure enough of itself to welcome and adapt ideas from other quarters. Syria was probably the main source of the raw material – elephants only became extinct there in the ninth century BC – and from Syria came impulses that had their sure effect on the evolution of Mycenaean ivory carving. Concepts that are obviously of Oriental provenance are the sphinx and griffin, and at least one theme was adopted by Mycenaean iconography – together per, haps with the religious concept – and that is the divinity hold, ing out the lifegiving plant to animal creation. In return the Oriental craftsmen adopted Mycenaean decorative patterns, portrayed subjects popular in Mycenaean art such as animal

Fig. 49. Ivory pyxis lid from Ras Shamra (after Kantor)

combats and bull scenes, and even received back their own original concepts as re-interpreted by Mycenaean artists. Sometimes we can distinguish Mycenaean ivory carvings actually imported by these eastern Mediterranean lands.

The art of painting is represented by the frescoes and the pottery. What survives of the former belongs mainly to the final period (LH III) and, of course, none of the frescoes is in its original position except for an occasional fragment at the base of a wall and the almost effaced decoration of the palace floors and hearths (the same technique was used for the floors as the walls). The art was inherited from the Minoans and underwent little change or development after being transplanted to the Greek mainland. Except for the Mycenaean outline technique and the addition of green to the colour range, there is little to distinguish the style of the latest Mycenaean frescoes from the painting in Crete of an earlier period. However, the subjects dictated by Greek taste were in the main different and reflected the energetic and warlike side of their character. Scenes of combat and of the chase

FRESCO
PAINTING

Plate 13

131

were preferred but these were by no means the only themes represented. Apart from the heraldic *tableau* behind the throne,
the varied activities of everyday life, both secular and religious,
were depicted. We see ladies gossiping in windows, horses

Plate 54

being groomed, a palace vista (all from Mycenae), and the
sport of bull-leaping (Tiryns). Some of the subjects are perhaps
mythological. One of these at Tiryns may represent Pandora's

Plate 38

box, and the lyre-player at Pylos is possibly Orpheus. Religious
scenes are represented by the fragmentary fresco of a shrine at
Pylos and the procession of genii with asses' heads from Mycenae. All these varied scenes were usually confined by an in-

Plate 47

tricate border of geometric patterns arranged in narrow horizontal bands. Sometimes this border decoration was dictated
by architectural considerations. Thus the 'triglyph' motive

Fig. 34

(see p. 129) provides a skirting for the walls of the Great Court
of the palace at Mycenae. Parts of this fresco are, or were, still
preserved *in situ*. Geometric designs filled the squares of the

Fig. 50

palace floors. Those used in the Great Court at Mycenae imi-
tated the graining of wood and the patterning of stone. Marine
motives are more prominent at Tiryns.

Much of the fresco-painting is executed in a hieratic style; the
figures of men and women are formalized and rather stiff, animals are more natural except when used heraldically. The skin
of the men is usually rendered in red and that of the women

Plates 38, 54

in white, a convention derived from Egypt via Crete. The
stylized symbols for rock, sky, and cloud were taken over from
the Minoans unchanged; so was the technique. The basic
foundation was a mud plaster applied to the wall of crude brick.
To this were added coats of plaster of finer texture. The paint
was then applied in true *fresco* technique, i.e. whilst the final
coat of stucco was still wet. Colours show little variation in
shade. The principal ones used were red, brown, orange, yel-
low, green, blue, grey and black. At Pylos it appears that the
whole picture was first sketched in orange and that details in

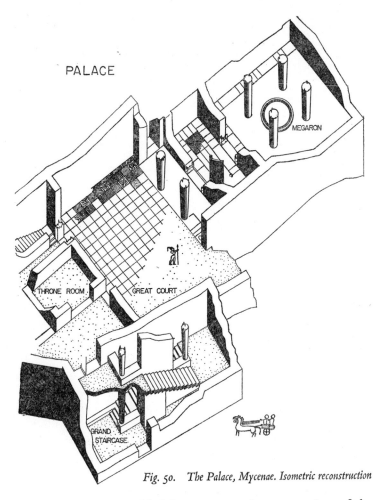

PALACE

MEGARON

THRONE ROOM

GREAT COURT

GRAND
STAIRCASE

Fig. 50. The Palace, Mycenae. Isometric reconstruction

other colours were added later. Hence the penetration of the
orange into the plaster is much deeper and the other colours are
inclined to flake off.

The influence of fresco-painting was an important factor in the
decoration of Mycenaean pottery in LH III. It is then that representations of man, animal, and bird start to appear on the
pottery. The chariot scenes and the antithetic animals portrayed

PAINTING
ON POTTERY
Plate 8
Figs. 12, 14, 52

on vases (see p. 54) undoubtedly take their origin from the frescoes. The development in pottery has been described in an earlier chapter. During LH III the style attained, and retained, a remarkable uniformity throughout the whole territory where, in the pottery was produced or exported. Though few kilns have been discovered – Tiryns and Berbati are two examples – it is often clear from the quality of the clay that the pottery was produced locally.

MYCENAEAN SOCIETY The wide distribution of its pottery bears witness to the might and fame of Mycenaean Greece in the ancient world, but concerning the form and organization of the society that created this pre,eminent position we know very little. The tablets provide some pointers towards an elucidation of this problem, but the value and interpretation of these are much debated. In Homer there are many references to relations between king and vassal and commoner, and between different kings, but these could perhaps reflect the system of government in force at the time he was writing (ninth/eighth centuries) and may not therefore be evidence for Mycenaean times. From Homer, archaeology, and the tablets together, we may build a picture of a number of kinglets and of one king having a higher status than the others; and such a position was most assuredly occupied by the lord of Mycenae, a city that archaeology has shown to have been richer and stronger than other cities. But the very geography of Greece makes it difficult for any one ruler to assert absolute and undisputed control over the whole mainland and still less over distant islands and colonies such as Rhodes and Cyprus. The mountains of Greece divide up the country into separate regions. Travel by land was often difficult, making it necessary to rely on communication by sea. Hence command of the sea was an important factor. It must have been the powerful fleet of the high king of Mycenae that ensured his foremost position, and the status of Pylos in that respect was not greatly inferior.

The meticulous records kept in the Palace of Nestor, and no doubt in all the other royal seats of power, give evidence of a highly organized bureaucracy, comparable to that of the great kingdoms of Egypt and Babylonia, from whom no doubt the Mycenaeans learnt the business. But it would be a mistake to translate systems of government, with which we are familiar, to Greek foreign waters. The methods would be imported but not the ideas. A certain similarity there must have been, for the very nature of bureaucracy is to superimpose its own character. From the tablets we learn of a hierarchical system, but the functions of the various office-holders are not always clear. At the head was the *wanax*, the king. This title is also applied to the gods, so that one may infer that the king was regarded as in some way sacred. Second to the king was the *Lawagetas*, Leader of the Host. He alone, besides the king, has his own *temenos* (the royal land-holding in Homer) and his own household. Next in line appear to be the *te-re-ta*, 'land-holders', a word that may be the same as Classical Greek *telestai* (the letters *l* and *r* are represented by a single series of signs in the script, see p. 37). Certain duties of the *te-re-ta* may have been connected with religious observances, and in Classical times *telestas* was also a religious title. Finally, there are the *hequetai*, the Followers (see p. 139).

References in the tablets to land tenure imply that the system was both communal and private. Some of the land was held in the name of the god. At Pylos, for instance, contributions were levied annually for Poseidon, the Earth-shaker. The word *basileus*, king, occurs frequently in the tablets, but it is clear that it has not the same meaning as in Classical times. The *basileus* seems to occupy a comparatively low grade in the social scale. In Homer, on the other hand there is apparently no distinction between *anax* (*wanax*) and *basileus*.

That slavery was a familiar institution is evident from the tablets. There are lists of women slaves, their occupation, and

SLAVES

their origin. Some of them are said to have come from Lemnos, Knidos, and Miletus, all situated on or near the west coast of Asia Minor. Miletus was a Mycenaean colony and the other two places were possibly trading posts. Slaves are also mentioned as coming from Kythera, just off the south coast of the Peloponnese. All of these places may have been slave markets.

TRADES AND CRAFTS
The distribution of labour, whether slave or native, is attested in some detail. The bronzesmiths, as befitted such a skilful trade – and one on which the fortunes of the army depended – enjoyed a special status. They were entitled to extra benefits in the form of taxrebates. Cabinetmaking was another specialized handicraft, and included inlaywork. Carding, spinning, and weaving were women's occupations. Other trades mentioned are those of saddler, seamstress, and perfumer. We know that rose, cyperus, and sage, with a base of olive oil, were used as ingredients in the making of perfumes. A physician is recorded once, but no details are given about his profession.

AGRICULTURE AND LIVESTOCK
That part of the economy which employed the greatest number would naturally be agriculture. This appears to have been highly organized, to judge from the numerous entries affecting this occupation: records of deliveries of land produce, taxes in kind due to the palace, a share set aside for some divinity, and so forth. The produce entered included wheat, barley, oil, wool. An elaborate system of assessment was employed for deliveries of wool. This seems to have been an important industry and a major source of wealth. Part would be used for local needs, but there must have been a large surplus available for export. Oxen are not recorded in great numbers. They seem mostly to have been used as draught animals and were obviously regarded with affection. In the tablets they are referred to by such pet names as Blondie, Dapple, Darkie, Whitefoot. At an early period an ox or an oxhide may have been a unit of measure in

Figs. 68, 69
barter. In LH III copper ingots were cast in the shape of an oxhide. They vary little in weight and it is quite possible that

Fig. 51. *Map of Argolis and Corinthia (after Wace and Stubbings)*

they were used as a rudimentary form of currency. A great hoard of them was found in the summer palace of Hagia Triada in Crete and recently a goodly number were recovered from the wreck of a Mycenaean ship off the south-west coast of

Turkey. Three examples are known from Sardinia (see. p. 160). The very comprehensive organization revealed by the tablets would be dependent to a great extent on a highly developed road system, an indispensable requirement for the promotion of trade and for the prosecution of war. Little of this system, naturally, has survived, but it can be traced in part from the ruins of prehistoric causeways and culverts that pass over small water-courses. The ruins of a causeway of almost Cyclopean construction can be seen today about a mile to the south of the Mycenae acropolis. It carried the road from Mycenae to the Heraeum (Prosymna) over the Chaos torrent. The road network has been studied principally in the area round Mycenae, but a valuable survey is in progress in Messenia. Two roads have been traced in part between Mycenae and Corinth, passing on either side of the mountain range that separates the two cities. These roads would have been guarded by forts along the route and perhaps toll was exacted for the use of them. A fort of this kind is situated on the summit of Mount Elias, one of the twin mountains that stand guard over Mycenae. In the *Agamemnon* of Aeschylus it is from the peak of this mountain that the signal fires announcing the fall of Troy are seen and the glad tidings brought to Clytemnestra.

CHAPTER VI

War and Trade

A STRONG IMPRESSION created by the monuments is of the dominant accent placed upon war by the Mycenaeans. It would almost seem as if they loved strife for its own sake. This element in their nature is conspicuous from the very first, as witness the rich and varied warlike equipment buried in the earliest of the Mycenaean tombs, the shaft graves. On the stelae that at one time marked the position of these graves chariot scenes are frequently recorded, in which the dead king triumphs over his foes. On fragments of a silver rhyton from Shaft Grave IV (see p. 127) the siege and assault of an enemy town are depicted, and from the many surviving pieces of fresco⁄paint⁄ing of a later period one knows that scenes of combat decora⁄ted the walls of the palaces. But the most impressive monu⁄ments of this warrior race are to be seen today in the great cita⁄dels of Mycenae and Tiryns.

Plate 20

Plate 59

The military aspect of the Mycenaean civilization is borne out by the tablets, particularly in regard to armaments. Of im⁄portance in the military sphere are the *hequetai*, the Followers, though their actual status is uncertain. They seem to stand close to the person of the king, perhaps as 'counts' did to the sovereign in the Holy Roman Empire. Chariots apparently were at their disposal and each one, according to a military tablet from Pylos, was attached to an *o⁄ka*; so it is supposed that they acted as in⁄telligence officers able to communicate information rapidly to royal headquarters. The *o⁄ka* was most probably a military unit but there is no agreement as yet as to its composition. In the context in which they appear they are referred to as 'guarding the coastal areas' presumably against a threatened invasion.

Fig. 52.   Chariot scene from a krater fragment, Mycenae (after Helen Wace)

The chariot figures prominently in the records both at Knossos and at Pylos, although in the case of the latter the reference is indirect, only chariot wheels being mentioned; these are described as being serviceable and unserviceable. The fact that the wheels are listed separately shows that they were dismounted from the chassis when the chariot was being 'garaged'. The reverse operation of mounting them is described by Homer: 'Swiftly Hebe put on the chariot the curved wheels of bronze...'; as a rule, however, the wheels were of willow or elm. The Knossos tablets give a full muster role: chariot, charioteer, his cuirass, and a pair of horses. The chariot carried two men, as is clear from frescoes, vase paintings, and seal-stones. The wheels are four-spoked and the axle is placed centrally under the carriage. A feature peculiar to the Aegean chariot is a stay running from the top of the carriage to the front end of the pole or shaft. It is joined to the pole by a series of thongs, and these connections are frequently reproduced in representations on vases.

Fig. 52

In the *Iliad* the chariot was merely a means of transport to bring the hero to the battlefield and to convey him swiftly thence, should the combat not end as heroically as anticipated. This is unlikely to have been its role in Mycenaean times, and an older tradition is hinted at in the *Iliad* when the sage Nestor describes the charge of a hundred chariots that took place in his father's time, something more akin to a cavalry charge. It was the use of such tactics and the possession of the chariot that no doubt enabled the otherwise peaceable Egyptians to build up an empire from the sixteenth century BC onwards. In Greece about this very time the earliest representation of a chariot ap-pears on the shaft grave stelae and we may suppose that it was this new instrument of warfare derived, it seems, from the Near East that assured the invaders of Hellas of ultimate dominion over the inhabitants. Similarly the use of the chariot may have been an important contributory factor in their conquest of Crete in the fifteenth century BC; at any rate the chariot first appears there about that time.

Plate 20

As the charioteer was unarmed, it is likely that the cuirass listed in the Knossos chariot muster-roll was intended for him. The

WEAPONS
AND
ARMOUR

Fig. 53.   Chariot tablet from Knossos (after Chadwick)

ideogram for a cuirass or coat-of-mail on the Knossos tablets is not the same as the one depicted on the Pylos tablets, neither is the word used for describing it. At Pylos the Classical word *thorax* is used and the ideogram bears some resemblance to the corslet portrayed on the Warrior Vase belonging to the end of the Mycenaean era. The Knossos cuirass, on the other hand, is remarkably like a bronze coat-of-mail recently found in a chamber tomb at Dendra (Midea), which is attributed to the transitional period LH II/III or the end of the fifteenth century, and this is but a little earlier than the presumed date of the Knossos tablets. This unique find reminds us of how much

Fig. 53

Fig. 54

Plate 7

Plate 65

Fig. 54. Pylos
corslet (after Ven-
tris and Chadwick)

Plate 7

Plate 56

Plate 64

must have perished of which we could have but little conception were it not for the record of the tablets. The later type of
corslet as shown on the Warrior Vase appears to be made of
leather, but the earlier kind on the Knossos tablets is specifically
stated to be of bronze. Bronze has a good chance of withstan-
ding the destruction of time but is is also a valuable metal and it
seldom escaped the attention of the tomb-robber.

There are two pieces of armour of which the tablets make no
mention, the shield and the greave. These are surprising omis-
sions, which are due no doubt to chance. Although no actual
example of a shield has survived, it is fairly well documented
from its representation on Mycenaean works of art. The Lion
Hunt dagger-blade from Shaft Grave IV shows two different
kinds of shield, the figure-of-eight and the 'tower' shield; the
latter is also portrayed in a battle scene on a gold signet ring
from the same shaft grave. The great size of these body-shields
precludes them from being made of anything heavier than leather and indeed it is known that the figure-of-eight shield was
made from an oxhide; this is apparent from the Fresco of
Shields, a recurrent theme in wall decoration which has been
found in the palaces of both Knossos and Tiryns; the dappled
design of the shields reproduces the colouring of the animal
hide. Crete seems to have been the home of this particular
model and perhaps of the 'tower' shield as well. On the mainland its use seems to have been confined to the sixteenth and
fifteenth centuries, but there are echoes of it in the *Iliad*, where
vague and ambiguous descriptions of this mighty shield hark
back to an old and almost forgotten tradition. In LH III, that
is, from the fourteenth century onwards, the whole Mycenaean
armoury undergoes a change. Contacts with the East increase
and influences from that quarter are reflected in new styles of
weapons both of offence and defence. The large body-shield,
which figured prominently in single combat and in the chase,
is now replaced by the small round shield that was better adapt-

ed to collective fighting. But as a sacred symbol and as an orna/
ment the figure/of/eight shield survived for at least another two
centuries. Two types of rounded shield are shown on the War/
rior Vase (LH IIIC), but there is doubt about their interpre/
tation. A circular shield, reminiscent of the kind used by the
Peoples of the Sea (see p. 174), is depicted on an LH IIIB
sherd. This type appears to have had a hand/grip but no
shoulder strap and in this respect it differed from the figure/of/
eight shield, which could be worn slung. As is shown on the
Warrior Vase, the shield was carried on the left arm. This fac/
tor was taken into account in the design of a Mycenaean for/
tress. At Mycenae (see plan) the main gate and the postern
gate are guarded by bastions so placed as to harass the unpro/
tected (right) side of an attacking force.

The 'well/greaved Achaeans' is a recurring phrase in the
Iliad, but up till now only two fragmentary examples of bronze
greaves have been found in chamber tombs belonging to the
end of the Mycenaean period, one in Cyprus and the other in
the north Peloponnese. The infantry on the Warrior Vase are
clearly wearing a leg protection of some sort and there are several
examples in fresco painting of men – soldiers or grooms – who
are obviously equipped in similar manner. It is likely that the
material was felt or leather. Bronze may have been substituted
during the later period, when the metal was cheaper and in
greater supply.

A purely Greek contribution to armour is the boar's tusk
helmet. It is fully described by Homer, yet this type of helmet
had gone out of use long before his day; it does not survive the
Mycenaean period. There are many illustrations of it in Myce/
naean art: it is worn by warriors depicted on gems and seal/
stones; it is a popular motive in ivory inlay work; it is figured
on the silver Siege Rhyton, but the most detailed version of it
takes the form of a warrior's head in ivory relief, usually
found in an LH III context. Its origin, however, goes back to

Plates 9,
63, 64
Plate 7

Plate 44
Fig. 35:
A, R

Plate 7

Fig. 39

Plate 62

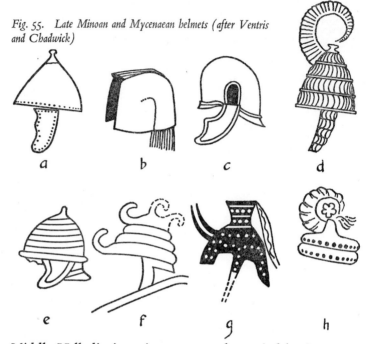

Fig. 55. *Late Minoan and Mycenaean helmets (after Ventris and Chadwick)*

a b c d

e f g h

Middle Helladic times, its most popular period having apparently been LH I and II. It was definitely an article of luxury, some thirty to forty pairs of boar's tusks being required to complete one helmet. Numerous fragments of these tusks have been found in tombs all over Greece. The boar's tusks, neatly cut into oblong plates and pierced at the shorter ends with holes, were sewn on to a frame of conical shape presumably of leather; the material has naturally not survived. The direction of the curve of the tusks was made to alternate in each successive row, of which there were generally four to five. This scheme is clearly reproduced in the ivory reliefs. The crown of the helmet was either adorned with a plume or terminated in a knob. Neck-guards and chin-straps are also shown in the ivory reliefs. Besides this helmet, several other types are known, but what was at one time thought to be a bronze helmet, found in a chamber

Fig. 55b

tomb at Dendra many years ago, is now believed to be the shoulder piece of a corslet of the LH II/III style referred to above. The latest kind of helmet is portrayed on the Warrior Vase, where two types are shown, one with horns and plume, the other ridged and crested. Both types seem to have been influenced by forms originating in the Near East. The white dots that decorate these helmets (and the corslets) on the Warrior Vase are generally interpreted as metal discs sewn on to the material, which was probably of leather or felt.

Plate 7,
Fig. 55g

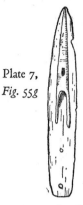

The main weapons of offence in the Mycenaean armoury were the spear, the sword, and the bow. The earliest style of spearhead is of unusual form and but sparsely represented. The bronze blade has a shoe-socket cast on one or both sides of it, into which the split point of the wooden shaft is inserted. Examples have been found at Sesklo, Levkas, Asine, and in Shaft Grave IV at Mycenae; it is of mainland origin. The more normal type of spearhead, in use throughout the whole of the Mycenaean age, was a narrow leaf-shaped blade with a strong mid-rib and a socketed base which was secured to the wooden shaft by a metal collar. The origin of this type seems to be Cretan. Several long, heavy spears of this kind were buried with the shaft-grave kings and its use with the chariot is depicted on the stelae. It is brandished in single combat in battle scenes portrayed on signet rings of the same period. It also appears as a weapon of the chase in the Lion Hunt dagger. Not many examples of it have survived from the latter part of the Mycenaean period but that it still retained its importance in warfare is confirmed by the fact that it is the only weapon portrayed on the Warrior Vase. There is very inconclusive evidence on the mainland for the light throwing spear, which plays such an important role in the Homeric epic.

Fig. 56. Shoe-socket spearhead (after Childe)

Fig. 56

Fig. 57

Plate 56

Plate 7

At the beginning of the Mycenaean period the most significant weapon of offence was the rapier, of which there are such abundant examples in the shaft graves, every warrior being

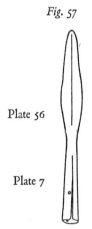

Fig. 57. Middle Minoan spearhead (after Childe)

145

equipped with a far greater number than he would have needed during his turbulent life. All are of fine workmanship and some of them richly and elaborately decorated, such as to suggest trophies rather than practical weapons. They have rounded shoulders, short tangs, and pronounced midribs which are usually semicircular in section. The forbears of this type (A) are certainly Minoan. But alongside these rapiers in the shaft graves is found another kind (Type B), less well represented than Type A and of which in the earlier Grave Circle there is only one example. The main difference between the two weapons is that Type B has square or pointed shoulders, a longer tang and a shorter blade. It may possibly have developed from the flanged dagger, of which there were several examples in the earlier Grave Circle, but it can also trace its ancestry to the Near East. A variant of Type B is the horned sword or rapier, the pointed shoulders being extended to form two horns. In the same way, although this is not certain, the cruciformshouldered rapier appears to be derived from Type A. The dagger is represented at this period by the beautiful examples from the shaft graves, justly renowned for their superb artistry. The intricate technique of gold, silver, and niello inlay owes its inspiration apparently to Asiatic and not Minoan work. During LH III a new type of sword was favoured, and again we must assume that this was due to broadening contacts with the Near East. The rapier continued in use in LH III A, as we know from finds datable to this period; but about this time it was being replaced by the twoedged or slashing sword as opposed to the thrusting style of weapon. One Mycenaean version of this new kind of sword has square shoulders; these, as well as the hilt, are flanged. The blade is broad with a widening towards the tip. It has no midrib. The earliest examples date from LH III A but probably to the latter part of it, that is to say, the second half of the fourteenth century. It is not clear from the tablets which kind of sword is indicated, as the drawings of them are so schematic.

Fig. 58

Fig. 59

Plate 56

Fig. 60

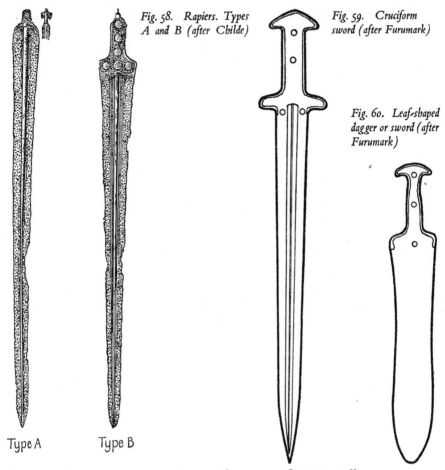

Fig. 58. Rapiers. Types A and B (after Childe)

Fig. 59. Cruciform sword (after Furumark)

Fig. 60. Leaf-shaped dagger or sword (after Furumark)

Type A   Type B

One example seems to portray the cruciform type of LH II. All of them are shown with a mid-rib and cannot therefore repre-sent the slashing sword, which would be unable to fulfill its function with such an impediment.

There are but few representations of the use of the bow in the archaeological record on the mainland and those few show exclusively scenes of the chase. The Lion Hunt dag-

Fig. 61

Plate 56

147

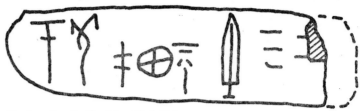

Fig. 61. Sword tablet (after Chadwick)

Fig. 62. Bronze arrowhead (after Ventris and Chadwick)

Fig. 65

Fig. 62

Plate 59

ger-blade is an example. From such sources, therefore, it could be assumed that the bow did not play an important part in Mycenaean warfare; but a fragment of a steatite vase from Knossos portrays a bearded archer who from his dress appears to be a Mycenaean, and at Knossos two large deposits of bronze arrowheads were found with tablet labels giving totals of 6,010 and 2,630 respectively. Bronze arrowheads are coupled with spearheads on the Pylos tablets. The bow, then, should be in-cluded in the Mycenaean armoury. Only the single-stave bow, or 'self-bow', is portrayed. There is no evidence to support the existence of the composite bow which is used by Odysseus in the slaying of the suitors. In LH I and II the arrowheads are made of flint or obsidian, usually with a hollow base so that their form recalls that of a bishop's mitre. They are beautifully fashioned. In LH III they are made of bronze and are often barbed. Archers as well as stone-slingers are depicted on the Siege Rhyton fragment, but these are not Mycenaeans but the enemy.

Brief mention should be made of the rowers listed on two Pylos tablets. There were more than 500 of them. This is our only reference to a possible navy. Representations of ships are few and very schematic (see p. 162). It is probable that the same kind of vessel was used for trade as for war (piracy).

TRADE

Fig. 63

At a very early stage in their history the Mycenaeans turned their attention towards the sea and far-off lands, inspired by a

spirit of adventure and a desire to add to the very limited resources with which nature had endowed their homeland. Already in the seventeenth century BC traces of Middle Helladic
influence can be seen in the designs on matt-painted pottery
produced in Sicily, and one matt-painted cup found in a
tomb at Monte Sallia in south-east Sicily is assuredly a MH
import. But the first evidence of early Mycenaean penetration
into this area comes from the Lipari Islands that lie to the
north of Sicily where a great number of potsherds have been
found, the majority of them painted in the style of LH I and II;
and matt-painted fragments that are transitional between MH
and LH I have been discovered on the island of Filicudi. At
Lipari itself the quantities of pottery are such as to suggest that
it was an important port of call for Mycenaean traders.

The island of Lipari is rich in the black volcanic glass known   OBSIDIAN
as obsidian which fractures like flint and can therefore be
easily turned into knife blades, scrapers, and other useful tools.
With great skill the Mycenaeans fashioned this material into
mitre-shaped arrowheads, some of them of extraordinary thin-
ness and delicate workmanship. Obsidian offered a cheap
source of readily produced implements of everyday use and
consequently was greatly sought after in ancient times. But it is
also found in the island of Melos and we may wonder why the
Mycenaeans should travel as far afield as Lipari to obtain their
needs when a readier source of supply was so close at hand;
Melos lies half way between Greece and Crete. But in the
early Mycenaean period this island was dominated by the
Minoans, who may not have been willing to share the obsidian
trade with outsiders and least of all with the growing menace
from the North. Certainly after the fall of Knossos Mycenaean
trade with Lipari is greatly diminished and this suggests that
the nearer source of obsidian was preferred from then on, but
one must also remember that in LH III bronze was being used
on an increasing scale and was becoming cheaper; obsidian

Fig. 63. Map of Europe and the Near East

GARY

kos

Thebes · Troy
·Chios

ANATOLIA

Samos
Miletus
Melos·
Knossos
C r e t e · Rhodes
C.Gelidonya·Vouni
Kition
Enkomi·

Cilic Tarsus
Mersin·i a Kazanli
Alalakh(TellAtchana)
Cyprus Ras Shamra
R.Orontes
Qatna
Byblos Syria

IRAN

Babylonia

Tell AbuHawam
Gezer· Lachish

·Cairo
Gurob·
EGYPT
Tell el Amarna·

H.A.S

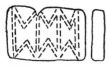

Fig. 64. Amber spacer beads from Mycenae (after Childe)

CONTACTS
WITH THE
WEST

Plate 57

Plate 20

Fig. 64

Fig. 65

arrowheads at this time were being replaced by that metal. And there can be no doubt that an important factor in the sea voy׳ages of the Mycenaeans was the search for the two metals that are used in the manufacture of bronze, i.e., copper and tin. Though tin constitutes but 10 % of bronze, it is very much rarer than copper and the nearest source to Greece in the Mediterranean seems to have been the tin mines of Etruria. It is significant therefore that LH III A potsherds, admittedly only four, have been found on the island of Ischia, on the route to Etruria. If pottery is a guide, the Mycenaeans sailed no further to the West than Ischia, but faint echoes of their influence reached as far as Britain. The Rillaton gold cup, if not a Mycenaean im׳port, resembles the horizontally fluted cup from Shaft Grave IV. It need not of course have been brought in a Mycenaean ship. But the so׳called Mycenaean dagger incised on one of the trilithons of Stonehenge is doubtful evidence. The hilt is unlike that of a Mycenaean dagger. There is perhaps some resemblance to the weapon engraved on one of the shaft grave stelae, which is certainly not a dagger and is probably a crude portrayal of the Type B sword (see p. 146) If, on the other hand, a Mycenaean inspiration of Stonehenge in its megalithic form is fanciful, a surer indication of trade relations between Britain and Mycenae is provided by the amber spacer׳beads found at Mycenae, Kakovatos, and Pylos, all of the fifteenth century, and these could well have borne the trade׳mark 'Made in England'. The Mycenaeans may even have prospected for tin in Cornwall, for, apart from the Rillaton cup, the fragment of a LH III sword (the 'Pelynt dagger') was found there in the tomb of a Wessex chieftain.

South Iberia was noted in antiquity for its tin and silver mines but evidence of Mycenaean contacts is not strong. Of pottery there is none. There are mitre׳shaped arrowheads that recall those found in the earlier Mycenaean tombs. From the dolmen of Matarrubilla come bone spacer׳beads that are very

Fig. 65.   Flint arrowheads from south Iberia (after Childe)

similar in many ways to ones made of paste and found in
Mycenaean tombs. The resemblance between the tholoi has
been noted and some scholars believe that the Greek tholoi are
derived from the Iberian ones, as the latter are mostly, if not all,
older. It is of course very probable that the Mycenaeans penetrated that far, but they have left little record – and that perhaps
indirect – of their wanderings. Mention should be made of the
segmented faïence bead. Great quantities of these were manufactured in Egypt round 1400 BC. They had a wide distribution:
not only have they been found in Spain but as far afield as
England and Brittany, the South of France, Hungary, and
several countries of Central Europe. Largely because of the far-
reaching extent of Mycenaean influence their dispersion has

Fig. 66

Fig. 67

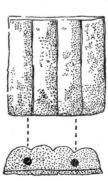

*Fig. 66.   Glass spacer bead from a chamber tomb, Mycenae
(after Wace)*

Fig. 67. Faïence segmented beads from Wiltshire (after Childe)

been attributed to Mycenaean initiative. The best evidence for this is that large numbers of these beads were found in the island of Salina (Lipari Islands), not in association with pot⸗ tery but with a great number of other beads of probable Myce⸗ naean manufacture.

Almost the only trace of Greek enterprise in Central Europe is the faïence segmented bead, if indeed the sale of this commod⸗ ity can be definitely attributed to the Mycenaeans. More re⸗ assuring evidence is provided by one or two pottery cups, made locally, that reproduce the Vapheio type with a fair degree of precision (one such cup comes from the Terremare in north Italy); and a gold cup from Fritzdorf, near Bonn, appears to imitate the form of a gold kantharos from the shaft graves. But it is more than probable that the Mycenaeans were prospect⸗ ing in these parts, for here were rich sources of copper. Another commodity that attracted the Mycenaeans was amber, which in the form of beads, often of exaggerated size, are so well re⸗ presented in the tombs of LH I and II. The amber came from Jutland and the route of this lucrative trade can be traced thence across Europe to the head of the Adriatic. In Greece the great⸗ est concentration of amber beads is along the west coast of the Peloponnese and so we may suppose that Greek ships had a share in the final transportation of this article, although there is no pottery evidence to support this assumption.

Relations with Egypt were active during LH I and II and several vases belonging to those periods have been found in tombs there. Most of them are of the alabastron type (see p. 48). But a much broader picture of relations with the Aegean is presented by the tomb paintings of the XVIII dynasty (fifteenth century) where the 'men of Keftiu' (Cretans) are shown bear⸗

Plate 66

EGYPT AND
THE AEGEAN
Plate 1

ing 'tribute' to the Pharaoh in the form of diverse vessels of gold
and silver, jewellery, copper ingots, textiles, and some articles   *Figs. 68, 69*
difficult to identify. The tomb of Rekhmere, vizier of Thoth-
mes III, which is some 40 years later than the earliest in the
series, may well fall within the period of Mycenaean domination of Crete. The ideograms on one of the Knossos tablets
show two bull's-head rhytons and a Vapheio-style cup that bear
a close resemblance to the portrayal of these objects in the Egyp-   *Fig. 70*
tian tombs. These are of metal, but the Vapheio cup was also reproduced in clay and countless examples of it have been found
in settlements and tombs, and no example known so far is
later than LH II. The richness and variety of the articles dis-
played in the Egyptian tombs is in strong contrast to what has
survived in actual fact; the textiles have naturally perished, the
precious and other metals have long since been looted and
melted down. This serves to remind us how inadequate is the
picture that we can reconstruct when we have to rely on the
few objects that have come down to us. In Greece all that can be
set against the 'tribute' to Egypt are a few scarabs of about this
period, some decorative motives in art (mediated through
Crete), and a large number of amethyst beads, the material of
which is believed to have been imported from Egypt. This
semi-precious stone was seldom worked in Greece after LH II.

Fig. 68.   *Wall painting from the tomb of Rekhmere, Thebes, Egypt (after Bossert)*

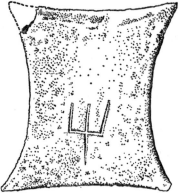

Fig. 69.   Copper ingot from Hagia Triadha (after Hood)

It is surprising that the few finds of Aegean pottery in Egypt at this period should be almost exclusively Mycenaean in view of the long tradition of friendly relations between Crete and Egypt and the greater proximity of that island. One can only conclude that the exports from the two Aegean powers were of a different nature. The route by which Greece conveyed this pottery to Egypt, with a hostile Crete athwart its path, would most likely pass through Rhodes. This island was one of the earliest of the Mycenaean colonies; it is geographically part of Asia Minor and well placed for trade with Syria and Palestine. A settlement was established in Rhodes at Triandha in LH II in the neighbourhood of a Minoan colony that had arrived a little earlier and enjoyed, it appears, a certain amount of independence from the mother country. Relations between the two communities seem to have been friendly at first – at least the Greeks were tolerated by the early comers. Later on, when the Mycenaeans had extended their power over the whole island, the Minoan settlement fades out of the picture. The pottery evidence shows that there was an even earlier Mycenaean contact at Miletus on the West coast of Asia Minor. Here too the Minoans had a colony that was destined to be superseded. But the route to Egypt follows the bulge of the Mediterranean

RHODES,
CYPRUS AND
THE LEVANT

and is marked out by the finding of LH II sherds at Tell Atchana, Ras Shamra, and Byblos in Syria and at Gezer and
Lachish in Palestine.

During LH III, after the fall of Knossos, the Mycenaean Age
reaches its full vigour and prosperity. Cos and other islands of
the Dodecanese come within the Mycenaean orbit. The settlement established in Rhodes spreads to embrace the whole
island, and the island of Cyprus, near the Syrian coast, is visited
in strength, it being rich in copper. These two islands spaced
away to the east from the Greek mainland enjoyed, as colonies
do, a certain amount of independence (though Cyprus was only
fully colonized towards the end of the Mycenaean era). The

*Fig. 70. Vapheio type cups
from an Egyptian tomb wall-
painting (after Childe)*

homogeneity of Mycenaean pottery throughout the Mediterranean argues for close relations with the homeland, but certain
individualities in style and vase-form develop in Rhodes and
Cyprus, and suggest that these islands had become centres of
production (though some scholars believe that all Mycenaean
pottery in the Levant was manufactured in Greece). The
differences are often subtle but sufficient for the trained eye to
detect Rhodian and Cypriot wares in Syria, Palestine, and
Egypt and even so far afield as Italy. For instance, to mention
the more obvious shapes uncommon in Greece, the krater
painted with pictorial scenes, the pilgrim flask, and the shallow   *Figs. 12, 13*
bowl occur in good numbers in each of the two islands and in
the Levant. Kylikes and deep bowls which are found so abun-   *Fig. 10*
dantly on mainland sites are rare in the other areas. Again, cer-

157

Fig. 71. Faïence lantern bead from a chamber tomb, Mycenae (after Wace)

tain vases have signs, interpreted as potters' marks, painted on the base, and these have a close affinity with the Cypro-Minoan script. Moreover, the forms of many of these vases are either native to Cyprus, or much favoured there. (Towards the end of LH III C the ceramic styles in both Rhodes and Cyprus diverge even more, foreshadowing the break-up of the Mycenaean world.)

MACEDONIA
THRACE
AND ASIA
MINOR

In LH IIIA and B, new areas are opened up to Mycenaean commerce and old trading stations developed. To the north and north-east pottery is exported to Macedonia, Thrace, and Troy. A great fortification wall is built to protect Miletus. The coast to the north of Cyprus bears witness to Mycenaean visita-tion. Although the potsherds so far found there are few (Mersin, Kazanli, Tarsus), one is reminded of the legend of Bellerophon and his immortal steed Pegasus that has Cilicia as its back-ground. The 'finger' of Cyprus points towards Ras Shamra; here and at Tell Abu Hawam on the Bay of Acre there were now important settlements, or so the large quantities of Myce-naean pottery from those sites would suggest. And trade was not confined to the coast but penetrated inland, particularly in Palestine. Except for one short and flourishing period, the pottery evidence from Egypt does not give any strong indica-tion of active trade with the Mycenaean emporia. The excep-tion is Tell el-Amarna where the heretic Pharaoh Akhenaten built his palace – not destined to outlast him. It was abandoned in 1350 BC, after which naturally no pottery was imported; therefore this date provides one of the few basic props for the framework of Mycenaean chronology. About 1,350 fragments were recovered from this site, representing perhaps some 800

Fig. 72. Rapier from Plemmyrion, Sicily (after Brea)

vases. A good percentage of them were pilgrim flasks that were Plate 1
quite possibly imported from Cyprus. It is to this short period
that a mutual interchange of ideas is to be attributed, profitable
to both parties. A new and freer spirit in Egyptian art was stimu-
lated at this time by the more intimate connections with the
Aegean, and Mycenaean design in arts other than pottery was
influenced by the exchange.

Though Rhodes and Cyprus play an important part in trade
with the Levant, the Greek mainland would be well represented. There is much from Greece to show that she was particularly interested in the Syrian trade. This includes storage jars
of Syrian manufacture, several faïence vases found at Mycenae
believed to come from that area, bronze statuettes of the thun-
der-god, Teshub (Mycenae, Tiryns, and Delos), a bronze axe
from the Vapheio tholos tomb, and cylinder seals. Then it is
almost certain that Syria was the source of the ivory that Mycenaean craftsmen carved with superb skill for the adornment
of caskets and furniture; and some of the motives and designs
on these ivories betray Syrian influence. A type of pendant
faïence lantern bead (fretwork technique and biconical in
shape) is possibly Syrian but it might equally well be of Mycenaean manufacture. It occurs in Greece, Rhodes, Cyprus,
Syria, *and* in Sicily.

Of necessity Greece's primary interest was centred in the Near SICILY
East, home of the most ancient civilizations; but the need for
expansion to maintain the standard of luxury to which she had
become accustomed led her further afield and principally towards the West. As we have noted, she already had a long-
standing connection with the Lipari Islands. The trade in that
area was maintained but on a reduced scale. It is now (LH III
A-B) that actual imports of Mycenaean pottery in Sicily appear, supplemented by Mycenaean jewellery including the lantern bead mentioned above. These are concentrated in the
south-east area of the island around Syracuse, a region that was

Fig. 72

to become one of the great centres of Magna Graecia in Archaic and Classical times. That there must have been earlier Mycenaean contacts here is attested by several rapiers of local manufacture that imitate shaft grave models. Legend associates Sicily closely with Crete. Minos is said to have been buried there. Diodorus's description of his tomb corresponds closely with the plan of the Temple-tomb of Late Minoan II (LH II) discovered at Knossos. And yet there is no sure evidence, certainly not pottery, of the Cretans ever having been in Sicily at all. But this paradox would find a partial solution if Minos (a royal title like Pharaoh) was a Greek! The locally made Sicilian pots are of coarse grey fabric and are known as Thapsos ware. (Thapsos is a promontory near Syracuse.) Some of the shapes of these vases show Mycenaean influence, but the decoration, which is incised, scarcely any. On the other hand, there are individual signs inscribed on a few of these pots from the Lipari Islands which bear some resemblance in certain cases to the Linear A script (see p. 31). As with the Cypriot vases mentioned above, they are probably potters' marks. Close to Sicily lies Malta. One LH III B kylix sherd is the only Mycenaean find from there so far.

SARDINIA

Sardinia in the Bronze Age was subject to many different cultural influences and one of these may have been Mycenaean. The island is dotted about with thousands of fortresses known as *nuraghi*. Many of them are of Cyclopean construction. The majority belong to a much later period, but at least one of them goes back to the fourteenth century according to radiocarbon dating. The art of Cyclopean building may therefore have been transmitted from Greece. No Mycenaean sherds have come to light on this island. On the other hand, three copper ingots of well-known form (they are shaped like an ox-hide) were found near Cagliari. On each of them is inscribed a sign: a double-axe, a trident, and an angular P. All these signs occur as potters' marks on the vases from Lipari referred to above, which are

Figs. 68, 69

thought to be in great part of Cypriot derivation. These particular ingots therefore may have originated in Cyprus, though one must not forget that a great hoard of ingots was found in the palace of Hagia Triada in Crete (at that time, however, the island was controlled by Mycenaeans). In 1960 another great hoard of ingots, also with signs on them, was recovered from the bottom of the sea from a ship that was wrecked off Cape Gelidonya. This is on the south coast of Turkey and lies between Cyprus and Rhodes. The implication is that this was a cargo from the Cypriot copper mines.

The extent of the connection with Sardinia must remain uncertain, but in the heel of Italy there is good evidence of Mycenaean interest in that area. Tradition relates that, after Minos's unsuccessful campaign against Sicily, in which he perished, remnants of the expedition took refuge in, and colonised, Apulia. The tradition concerning the identity of the survivors is apparently belied, unless they had Rhodian allies, by the considerable quantity of Mycenaean pottery found at Taranto of which certain pieces are quite definitely Rhodian; Cyprus is also represented there. Taranto, or Taras as it was called in Classical times, was colonised in 706 BC and was the capital of Magna Graecia in Italy, but its original foundation goes back to the fourteenth century. That from the pottery evidence seems to be the date of the first Mycenaean settlement. From there, it appears, a flourishing trade was conducted with the north of Italy (the Terremare) and the products from that area were transmitted to Greece. The evidence for this is not very strong, but Terremare bronzes have been found at Taranto (and nowhere else in the south of Italy) and a mould for making a winged-axe of Terramara type was uncovered in Mycenae. The bronze-smith who used this mould may have been a Mycenaean who learnt his skill in north Italy or a travelling Terramara bronze-smith who worked at Mycenae. In either case there was a close connection.

SOUTH AND NORTH ITALY

Fig. 73

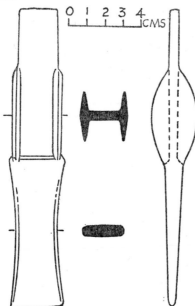

Fig. 73. Reconstruction of a casting from a mould found at Mycenae (after Stubbings)

SEA ROUTES
AND SHIPS

There is little definite that can be said about Mycenaean ships or the routes they took. In the Aegean where land is seldom out of sight there was no problem, but the sea voyage to the West is more precarious. In Classical times the route to Italy and Sicily was by the Ionian Islands, that is, up the west coast of Greece as far as Corfu and across the narrowing of the Adriatic. Very much the same route is followed today and no doubt the Mycenaeans used it too. The earliest representation of a ship is found very suitably on a Middle Helladic vase fragment from Iolkos in Thessaly, for it was there according to legend that the Argo was built and from there that Jason and the heroes sailed in quest of the Golden Fleece, to the far-off Caucasus. The Iolkos ships – two of them are portrayed – are fragmentary and sketchy, but it can be seen that even at that period they had a ram (a prolongation of the keel), as was later the case in post-Mycenaean times. The ship could therefore be used for war and

Fig. 74

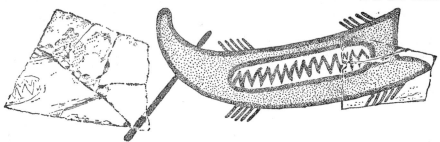

Fig. 74.   Reconstruction of a ship from fragments of a Middle Helladic vase from Iolkos (after Theochares)

piracy as well as for trade. Oars are indicated and as with other craft of the period, for example, Egyptian, there is a great oar rudder at the stern. Representations on seal-stones and later vases show that there was a cabin and, as was to be expected, a sail. The draught was shallow and consequently the ship could be beached in wind-protected, sandy harbours. It is unfortunate that the wreck off Cape Gelidonya cannot add further details to this meagre account. Only a small part of the hull, caught in a cleft, survived. Most of the ship and its contents had been swept away by strong currents. The principal cargo, as we have seen, was copper which on account of its great weight (half a ton) was not easily moved by the waters. With it were found bronze tools, a few scarabs, a cylinder seal from Syria, basketry (deep water is a wonderful preservative), domestic pottery, and part of the crew's dinner (inevitably fish!). The wreck is probably to be dated to the latter part of the thirteenth century.

What had the Mycenaeans to offer in exchange for the goods of other countries to enable them to accumulate such vast wealth? In terms of archaeology we know of the copper mines of Cyprus. An ancient copper mine, but of unknown antiquity, has been discovered at Nemea to the north of Mycenae, and there are lead mines at Laurion in Attica, which may have been worked in Mycenaean times. Gold mines may also have existed but of these today there is no trace in Greece. Mycenaean gold is generally believed to have come from the Egyptian pro-

SOURCES OF WEALTH

vince of Nubia. Egyptian gold may have been earned by mer-
cenaries fighting for Pharaoh Ahmose for the liberation of his
country from the Hyksos in the sixteenth century. Undoubtedly
straightforward robbery, dignified by the name of trade, played
a part. With piracy go tolls, protection money and the like.
But all of this is conjecture. The tablets can perhaps provide
some clue. The philologist, John Chadwick, has made an in-
triguing analysis of some of the texts. He has emphasized the
importance of the wool tablets at Knossos that testify to production on a very large scale, and we may recall the 'tribute' of
textiles from the Keftiu portrayed in the Egyptian tombs. On
the Pylos tablets there is frequent mention of flax, *ri-no* (*li-non*,
from which is derived our word, linen) and it is grown in
Messenia to this day. From archaeology alone we could only
have the most indirect evidence of such commodities. Again,
Chadwick points out that the number of smiths employed at
Pylos and the quantities of bronze allocated were far in excess
of the requirements of the palace. Was the bronze being pro-
cessed for export? The slave-trade may have provided an important source of income (see p. 135). Each of the three sites that
have produced tablets refers to spices and this is of some significance. Spices were of considerable importance in antiquity
and particularly in the form of unguents which were in demand
by both sexes. The Mycenae tablets from the House of Sphinxes give the most complete list of ingredients used. (One in particular, coriander – the word has remained almost unchanged

Plate 2

throughout the ages – provided a useful check in the decipherment). 'Unguent-boilers' are quite frequently mentioned and
one of the most suitable vessels for dispensing an oily substance
is the stirrup-jar. Numerous examples of this jar occur in the
Levant and especially at Tell el-Amarna. It is perhaps of some
significance that few stirrup-jars have been found in the backward areas of the central Mediterranean they are very commonly found in civilised centres.

All the great civilizations of the Near East–Egypt, Babylonia, the Hittites – had built up their great wealth from their own natural resources with which they had been happily endowed; they did not have to "export or die". But Greece has always been a poor country; its wealth has lain in the ingenuity, talents, and industry of its people. To compete with its neighbours it has had to turn these energies outwards. The rise to power and affluence of the Mycenaean civilization can be compared to the ascendancy of the Venetian republic whose prosperity was also founded on commercial enterprise. The analogy is only intended to emphasize that it was the same driving force behind the two cultures that raised them both from a humble status to a position of unimagined wealth and power. They differed widely in their political background.

CHAPTER VII

Rise and Fall of Mycenae

A RCHAEOLOGY CAN PROVIDE the broad outlines of the rise and fall of a great civilization but by itself it is only able to give an anonymous record. The epics of Homer and many legends recounted by later authors are now generally recognized as having a historical foundation. They can be used to breathe life into the dull, scientific record, but is is not always easy to relate the archaeological facts to legendary persons and events. Any historical reconstruction of this kind must be tentative and in many cases different interpretations are possible. The Homeric epics in general, and many of the legends, speak of two heroic periods. In a very broad sense the earlier cycle can be assigned to the LH I and II periods and the second cycle to the latter part of LH III, but there will always be exceptions to any generalised rule.

When the Mycenaeans first appear on the scene in the early sixteenth century, the finds from the shaft graves show that their culture was already rich and complex. It exhibits evident signs of many and varied contacts with the outside world: amber from the North, obsidian perhaps from Lipari, ivory from Syria, gold presumably from Egypt, and – an invisible import – the Minoan impress on the artistic treasures in the tombs. The Cretan influence is more noticeable in Grave Circle A; the earlier Grave Circle B has a much larger percentage of Middle Helladic pottery. No constructions on the Citadel at Mycenae can be definitely related to this period. Later rebuilding of the palace has removed all recognizable trace of them. Perseus, a mythological rather than legendary figure, is the traditional founder of the city. Pausanias says, 'that Perseus became the builder of Mycenae, the Greeks know,' but this need not mean that he built the Cyclopean walls, which belong to LH III.

On the evidence of the late MH pottery found in the Kardit-sa and Koryphasion tholoi (see p. 79) it is probable that Iol-kos and Pylos were two other Mycenaean centres that were flourishing in LH I. According to legend, there was some connection between the two areas at this time. Pelias and Ne-leus were twin brothers whose home was Iolkos. They quar-relled, and Neleus was compelled to migrate to Messenia where he founded a dynasty. His famous son, Nestor, was one of the heroes of the Trojan war. Pelias's half-brother was Aison, the father of Jason, who sailed in the Argo in quest of the Golden Fleece. This would have been an expedition to the Black Sea, but unfortunately it has left no archaeological trace. However, at this time, or a bit earlier, the Mycenaeans were already voy-aging far and wide. LH I and II vases are found at Troy and Miletus and in the West in the Lipari Islands, where they had already been preceded by their Middle Helladic forefathers. In LH II a settlement is established in Rhodes and from this base trade was developed with the Levant and Egypt.

The powerful realm of Minos lay athwart the direct route to Egypt and not until this dreaded rival was overcome could the Mycenaean kingdoms, among which we may count at this time Mycenae, Pylos, Iolkos, and probably Thebes and Orcho-menos, enjoy undisputed sway over the Mediterranean. The beginning of the great period of Mycenaean hegemony appears to coincide with the destruction of Knossos in the first half of the fourteenth century. The exact date of the catastrophe is uncertain, but is was apparent to certain scholars from the archaeological evidence alone that Mycenaean influence, if not a Mycenaean buccaneer prince, was already strongly esta-blished in the Minoan capital before it was destroyed. Ad-mittedly a good part of the argument was based on the military character of some of the tablets, the date of which has been challenged by some scholars; but there was other evidence in-dependent of the tablets that supported this theory. There were the great Palace Style jars found only in Knossos and East Crete, whereas these vessels, and they are in the majority, are known from many sites on the Greek mainland. Several tombs of this period (LM II) reproduce the plan of the Mycenaean chamber tomb and from their contents have merited the title of 'Warrior Graves'. Such graves are foreign to Minoan tradition. Moreover, one style of vase appears in these tombs that was never popular in Crete, the alabastron (see p. 48). Great quantities of them are found on the Greek mainland, but only a very limited number in the realm of Minos. Finally, there is a tholos near Knossos of pure Mycenaean construction and design; it shows little affinity with the earlier vaulted tombs of southern Crete.

The Greeks who dominated Crete at the end of the fifteenth century, while imposing their own predilections in burial customs and for certain types of vases, did not materially influence the existing, older and more advanced, Minoan culture. They received more than they gave. They learnt the art of writing and the benefits arising therefrom, including efficient, albeit bureaucratic, organization; and from Minoan Linear A was developed Mycenaean Linear B.

Whoever inherited or usurped the revered title of Minos was a power to be reckoned with in the ancient world. Is it to this period that Minos's disastrous expedition to Sicily is to be assigned? A restless, ambitious, and adventurous Greek might well have attempted such an undertaking. The story relates that Minos went to reclaim Daedalus, the architect of the Labyrinth at Knossos, who had taken refuge in the court of King Kokalos in southern Sicily and there carried out many important engineering works for his new master; obviously a Leonardo da Vinci, whose services could ill be dispensed with. Minos perished in Sicily and the remnants of his ill-fated expedition settled and colonized Apulia in the heel of Italy. The archaeological evidence is ambiguous for the earlier periods (sixteenth and fifteenth centuries), but in the fourteenth century the influence in Sicily is unmistakably Mycenaean and noticeably so in southern Italy, where a Rhodian element can be recognized. Then there is the famous episode of Theseus and the Minotaur, indicating that Athens was tributary to Knossos for a while; and this is perhaps borne out by the recent excavations at Keos, an island off the coast of Attica, where many vases of LM I and II, coinciding with this period, have been found. The legend implies that Athens cast off the Minoan yoke. Was that city the leader in a revolt that was to crush a detested Mycenaean rival? Was not the moment perhaps opportune after the failure of the Sicilian expedition? Greeks were ever at war with one another in the Classical period and may have been equally antagonistic in earlier times. All we know is that Greeks in Knossos in the fourteenth century succumbed to an envious power and that after that there is rather more evidence of Mycenaean influence there although the basic culture is always able to maintain its distinctive Minoan character. As an example of antagonism between Greeks in prehistoric times one may recall the famous war of the Seven against Thebes. This unsuccessful expedition, in which the sons of Oedipus perished, was organized principally from the Argolid. The succeeding generation, the Epigonoi, accomplished their objective and Thebes was destroyed – in the same generation as the fall of Troy according to tradition. The date does not accord with the archaeological evidence. As the modern town of Thebes covers the ruins of the old, very little excavation has been possible, but it seems to suggest that the palace was destroyed at the beginning of the fourteenth century BC. The town, however, must have been reoccupied later, for there are many tombs of the latest Mycenaean period (LH IIIC).

A round figure for the effacement of Knossos is 1400 BC, though from the pottery evidence its destruction seems more likely to have taken place 30 to 50 years later. But whatever the exact date, it marks the beginning of the most flourishing period of the Mycenaean civilization. The cargoes from the Greek mainland circulate unchallenged throughout the Mediterra, nean, at least as far as Ischia in the West. The Cyclades, and notably Melos, bear the imprint of Mycenaean colonization. Trade with Egypt reaches its height during the brief reign of Akhenaten. There are mercantile settlements in Cyprus, from which the Levant markets are exploited. Rhodes, colonized in the previous century, acquires a semi-independent status; it has its own trading station in far-off Taranto. At Mycenae itself a new dynasty assumes power, the Pelopids. Pelops, the founder, is said to have come from Asia Minor. This in itself is indica, tive of the spirit of the times when any adventurous prince within the Mycenaean realm might hope on some fictitious claim, like William the Conqueror, to carve out a kingdom for himself, and best of all to establish himself in the seat of power; for Mycenae, though it might be accounted *primus inter pares*, was the most powerful of the Mycenaean kingdoms, and this is confirmed by the archaeological evidence.

But it is just about this time that historical records make some contribution towards the meagre information afforded by arch, aeology and legend. In the annals of the Hittite emperors of the fourteenth and thirteenth centuries mention is made of a Kingdom of Ahhijawa. Though there are certain philological difficulties in the equation Ahhijawa: Achaea, the identifica, tion is accepted by most scholars. In Homer the Greeks fre, quently call themselves Achaeans and no doubt they did so in Mycenaean times also. The Hittites in their documents, on the other hand, referred to countries rather than peoples. In the case of Ahhijawa it is clear that they refer to a sea power. A most important document is a long, and on the whole conciliatory, letter addressed by the Hittite emperor to the King of Ahhijawa who at that time appears to have been in the vicinity; and for that reason it has been supposed by some scholars that Ahhi,

awa must be Rhodes, one of the most powerful of the Mycenaean kingdoms, as we have seen. But there can be no question
that the real centre of power was at Mycenae, to which the monuments in the Argolid, surpassing all others in Greece, bear
witness. The Hittites, being a land and not a sea power, could
have little knowledge of the territory that constituted the Achaean dominion or where its centre of gravity lay. Contact was
limited to the areas where the two realms touched. In the
present instance – the occasion of the letter referred to above –
this was Millawanda (or Milawata) which is generally supposed to be the same as Miletus. A boundary dispute? Not altogether, but it emerges from the letter that Miletus and its
hinterland were at that time part of Mycenaean territory, though
temporarily occupied by the Hittite emperor. This suggests
that the line of demarcation between the two powers was somewhat fluid. It has already been noted that Mycenae had a long
trading connection with Miletus and later on had a colony
there. It also had trading relations with Mersin and Kazanli
in Cilicia, and a settlement at Ras Shamra. All these with the
exception of the last-named are just inside the Hittite border,
and Ras Shamra itself is close to the frontier. The two realms
therefore touched very closely but it can be inferred from the
Hittite archives that relations between them were on the whole
friendly, each recognizing its own limitations: the one all-
powerful on land, the other in control of the seas.

On the eve of the Trojan War the might of Mycenae pervaded the whole of the central and eastern Mediterranean, but
there is evidence that it had already passed its zenith. About the
middle of the thirteenth century the capital city suffered some
incursion that destroyed houses outside the citadel and these
were never rebuilt (see p. 100). The citadel itself may have
suffered to some extent at this time. In any event, after this disas-
ter the fortification walls were extended and the secret cistern
built (see p. 107). Whether this attack on the citadel is to be

attributed to a civil war, the enmity between the brothers, Atreus and Thyestes, sons of Pelops and rival claimants to the throne, there is no means of telling. It may equally well have been the first of a series of attacks that were ultimately to over-whelm the principal fortresses on the Greek mainland. Many of these appear to have been reinforced about this time, and a little later, towards the end of LH IIIB, a massive wall, Cy-clopean-built, was constructed at the Isthmus of Corinth to ward off an expected attack from the North. Parts of this wall are preserved to this day at the south-east end of the isthmus.

It is not certain whether this unsettled state of affairs on the mainland preceded the ambitious expedition against Troy or was subsequent to it; nor is it clear what was the cause of the war, for the abduction of Helen by a prince of Troy was merely used as an excuse. Troy had enjoyed a period of almost un-broken prosperity for centuries. The basis of her wealth has been variously assessed. Trade may have contributed a good part of it, but her connections were exclusively with the West. In spite of bordering the great empire of the Hittites on the north-west, she received no recognizable Hittite imports. The city, however, was not dependent on trade alone. Unlike the barren mountainous home of the Mycenaeans with its infre-quent fertile valleys, the rich, productive plains of Troy (the Troad) provided ample food for the inhabitants and more to spare. The country, according to Homeric poems, was famed for its horses. Moreover, Troy had a thriving spinning and presumably weaving industry. The quantities of spindle whorls found there far exceed those discovered on any other site. Hence, the city may have been a serious competitor to the Mycenaeans in the textile trade (see p. 164). And the time may have seemed to them opportune for an attack, for about 1300 BC (end of Troy VI) the city was shaken by a devastating earthquake, from the effects of which it recovered only gra-dually. (A few scholars identify this catastrophe with the fall of

Homeric Troy, although there is no evidence of destruction by fire.) One can only speculate. Against this rival, considered formidable, gathered all the might of Greece with Agamemnon, 'king of men' as the poet describes him, at its head. The impressive array of kings and princes that followed him is recorded in the Catalogue of Ships (see p. 43). The war was long drawn out. Many heroes fell and many of those who returned to their homeland found much tribulation on the way. It seems to have been a Pyrrhic victory.

Whatever date be given for the fall of Troy VIIa – some would place it as high as 1260 BC and others prefer to accept Eratosthenes's date of 1184 BC (a date that is by no means sacrosanct) – it occurred before the end of LH IIIB, for vases in that style were still being imported when this city was reoccupied after its terrible devastation. But the end of LH IIIB also marks the destruction of many of the great citadels on the mainland, Mycenae, Tiryns, Midea, Pylos. Others such as Gla, Zygouries, Prosymna, Berbati, Korakou, were either abandoned or destroyed at this time. The highly-organized expedition against Troy could not conceivably have been undertaken after these disasters and must have preceded them by several decades if any credence is to be given to Homeric and later traditions. In the *Odyssey* we are able to follow the fate of many of the heroes who survived the Trojan War. Agamemnon returned to Mycenae and was treacherously murdered by Clytemnestra aided by Aegisthus, his cousin, who then reigned for eight years in his stead. Orestes, son of Agamemnon, avenged his father's death and assumed the throne. Nestor returned to Pylos and later tradition relates that he was succeeded by his son and grandson. All then depends upon the dating of IIIB pottery which was being produced in Pylos till its final destruction. If it went out of fashion around 1200 BC at Pylos, the fall of Homeric Troy must have taken place some decades earlier (unless we assume with some scholars that Troy was destroyed

by invaders other than the Greeks and in that case Eratosthenes's date is irrelevant). But if the LH IIIB style of pottery
lasted longer, as it may well have done in certain areas, it is still
not possible to accept the Greek traditional date of 1184 BC; for
other momentous events in the eastern Mediterranean, which
have some bearing on this period and are documented both by
pottery and Egyptian records, would not admit of so late a date.

About 1225 BC restless migratory forces, referred to as the
'Peoples of the Sea' in the Egyptian annals, were threatening
the western Delta. They were defeated by the Pharaoh Mernep-
tah, successor to Rameses II. The names of the peoples taking
part are listed and among them certain scholars identify the
Danaans and the Achaeans, both names used by Homer for the
Greeks. These interpretations present certain philological difficulties. Be that as it may, the Peoples of the Sea reappear some
30 to 40 years later, greatly augmented in strength, and this time
they attack Egypt from the east. The trail of their maraudings
can be traced along the south coast of Asia Minor and the
littoral of the Levant. Cyprus may have been devastated by
them at this time. Alalakh (Tell Atchana) and Ras Shamra in
north Syria fell to the invaders and Mycenaean IIIB pottery is
found among the ruins. But once again they were repulsed on
the borders of Egypt, and this time decisively, by Rameses III
in 1191 BC (or 1186 BC according to others. Egyptian dates at
this period are liable to a discrepancy of up to ten years). Among
the defeated tribes were the Peleset (Philistines), who thereafter
settled in Palestine. Shortly after they had established themselves
in their new home, 'Philistine' ware appears and this has strong
affinities with the Mycenaean IIIC style pottery being produced in Cyprus after its visitation (by the Peoples of the Sea?)
referred to above. Now, this style of pottery originated at Mycenae after the disasters that overtook the Greek mainland and
these cannot have taken place much later than 1200 BC if a
modified version of the new (IIIC) style pottery was to reach

Palestine via Cyprus shortly after 1191 BC. On these grounds, therefore, a date of 1260–50 BC for the Fall of Troy is preferred.

If the above account appears confusing, this is unavoidable, for the times themselves were confused and disturbed. Tribes were on the move, perhaps driven from their distant homelands by famine. For the Peoples of the Sea it was a mass migration. They brought their families and belongings with them and thus they are graphically depicted on the Egyptian monuments. The Hittite empire disintegrated in their path. Egypt was scarcely able to withstand the invaders, and now came the turn of the Mycenaeans. But the danger to them seems to have come not from the sea but the land. The sea after all was their element, and it should be noted in passing that the Cyclades and the Dodecanese appear not to have been affected by the upheaval. In fact, Rhodes at this time was still trading with far-off Taranto and was exporting to Attica and western Anatolia (Turkey). The indications are that the threat to the mainland came from the north, and according to a very strongly held Greek tradition Greek tribes known as the Dorians came down from the north and overran the Peloponnese two generations after the Fall of Troy. This event is picturesquely referred to by the ancient sources as the Return of the Heraclidae. Hyllos, a son of Heracles, slew Eurystheus, the last of the Perseid kings of Mycenae (and the one who had imposed the famous Twelve Labours upon his father), but Hyllos himself was later slain in a battle between the Heraclidae and a Peloponnesian force led by Atreus, son of Pelops, who had succeeded to the throne of Mycenae. The Heraclidae retired and were forbidden by the Delphic oracle to return for another 80 years. The legend has been interpreted by some as a series of onslaughts by the Dorians against the Peloponnese, the first of which would have been halted at the Isthmus; perhaps by the great Cyclopean wall referred to above, or it may be this wall was built as a result of the attack.

The Dorians have left no archaeological trace. No pottery, jewellery, weapons, or burial customs can be assigned to them. A few scholars even doubt their existence but there is the Doric dialect to attest their presence (see p. 24). Their culture was either non-existent, inferior, or a debased form of Mycenaean. They were possibly a nomadic tribe. The ultimate success of these invasions – if they are to be attributed to the Dorians – may have been due to the connivance of a discontented and ambitious nobility, for the Cyclopean-built fortresses, could only succumb to starvation or treachery. Athens alone of all the Mycenaean strongholds held out, and it was the proud boast of later Athenians that they were an autochthonous people and had repelled all foreign invasion; and indeed archaeology seems to bear out their claim. But although there are no signs of destruction on the Athenian acropolis at this time (*c.* 1200 BC), earlier habitation near the foot of it was now left derelict and the succeeding period shows signs of impoverishment. At this time there was also a movement of people to the east coast of Attica.

In the Peloponnese there was a general dispersion of population. Some went overseas to start a new career in Cyprus – whether as friend or foe is not known; others went further afield to Tarsus – and there is a legend that Amphilochus settled in Cilicia after the Trojan War. Achaea on the north shore of the Peloponnese was now occupied and perhaps for the first time in any great strength, for the pottery from the tombs (our only evidence) is predominantly in the LH IIIC style. After the sack of Pylos, which may have suffered a sea as well as land invasion, many of the inhabitants of Messenia took refuge in the neighbouring Ionian islands and particularly in Cephalonia.

In all these areas, both in the east and west Peloponnese, IIIC pottery (twelfth century) was now being produced exclusively, and the centre of this new style, of which the finest kind is the so-called Close Style, appears to have been My-cenae. Mycenae alone of all the great citadels in the Pelopon-nese was reoccupied, though on a much reduced scale. Once more it took the lead, either under new overlords or because it finally succeeded in repelling the earlier onslaughts. Its domin-ion was almost co-extensive with the old, but the bonds of control were loosened and the commonalty impoverished. As evidence for the former we have the local divergencies of style in III C pottery, specially notable in Achaea and Cephalonia; and for the latter, the abandonment of settlements in the Argolid and the debased standard of workmanship. No Linear B tab-lets are known from this period and it seems likely that the old system of records and control had broken down to give way to a more primitive form of government. A growing deterioration in the quality and design of the pottery is apparent, and to-wards the end of the period the simple and crude Granary style (see p. 54) becomes increasingly popular. It is the style that was very much favoured in Cyprus after that island suffer-ed a second and major destruction some time before 1100 BC; and it suggests that the attack came from the Greek mainland and was followed by actual settlement, for chamber tombs of Mycenaean type are now introduced into the island for the first time.

Turmoil and unrest were once more returning to the Myce-naean world. The negative evidence for this is the abandon-ment of many cemeteries before the end of the period. Cist burials supersede chamber tombs in Attica, the Argolid, and Boeotia. Single or double interments replace multiple burial and there is anthropological evidence of a new ethnic element in the population. The origin of the cist tomb cannot be traced, unless it be a revival from Middle Helladic times, but the con-tents of the tomb, other than the pottery which reflects the old tradition, are no longer Mycenaean. Long bronze pins and fibulae (an elaborate safety-pin) are now fashionable; the ubiquitous Mycenaean figurine (see p. 70) disappears. But these changes were preceded by catastrophes that mark the end of Mycenaean power and its civilization. They are not on the scale of the previous disasters, perhaps because there was less to destroy. In the north, Iolkos, the capital of the kingdom of Thessaly, was overwhelmed. At the eastern extremity of the realm, Miletus was burnt down and, at the very centre of all, Mycenae was finally destroyed. A round date for all these cala- mities would be in the region of 1100 BC. The IIIC phase is a melancholy period. The Mycenaean polity never really re- covered from the onslaughts made on it at the end of the thir- teenth century. The elaborate administration that had main- tained its power disintegrated, its trade which was its life-blood was disrupted and the fabric of its society decayed to an inglori- ous end. We are on the threshold of the Dark Ages.

Bibliography

Abbreviations

AJA   *American Journal of Archaeology.*

Archaeological published by the Council of the Society for the Promotion
  Reports   of Hellenic Studies and the Managing Committee of the
          British School of Archaeology at Athens.

Archaeology   published by the *Archaeological Institute of America.* New
          York.

BSA   *Annual of the British School at Athens.*

CAH   *Cambridge Ancient History.* Revised edition of Vols. I, II.

Expedition   *Expedition.* The Bulletin of the University Museum of the
          University of Pennsylvania. Philadelphia. 1961.

Hesperia   *Hesperia. Journal of the American School of Classical Studies at
          Athens.*

JHS   *Journal of Hellenic Studies.*

Klio   *Klio. Beiträge zur alten Geschichte.* Leipzig.

General

Archaeology 13; 1. (1960). A number that is devoted entirely to Mycenaean Civilization.

H.T.BOSSERT. *The art of ancient Crete.* London. 1937. Includes a section on the Greek mainland, but is mostly a picture book.

SIR ARTHUR EVANS. *The Palace of Minos.* London. 1921–35.

D.FIMMEN. *Die kretisch-mykenische Kultur.* Berlin. 1924.

G.GLOTZ. *La civilisation égéenne.* Paris. 1953.

S.N.MARINATOS and M.HIRMER. *Crete and Mycenae.* London.1960.

F.MATZ. *Crete and Early Greece.* London. 1962.

—. *Kreta, Mykene, Troja.* Stuttgart. 1956.

M.P.NILSSON. *Homer and Mycenae.* London. 1933.

L.R.PALMER. *Mycenaeans and Minoans.* London. 1961.

STUART PIGGOTT, editor. *The Dawn of Civilization.* London. 1961.
  Chapter VII. *The Home of the Heroes* by M.S.F.HOOD.

F. SCHACHERMAYER. *Die ältesten Kulturen Griechenlands*. Stuttgart. 1955.

C. TSOUNTAS and J. I. MANATT. *The Mycenaean Age*. London. 1897. A comprehensive survey. Out of date but still valuable.

A. J. B. WACE. *Mycenae: An archaeological history and guide*. Princeton. 1949.

A. J. B. WACE and F. H. STUBBINGS. *A Companion to Homer*. London. 1962.

T. B. L. WEBSTER. *From Mycenae to Homer*. London. 1958

The following is a list of the principal and important book publica-tions on Mycenaean excavations. It is necessarily selective. Those that are numbered are referred to again in the bibliography under the different chapter headings.

1. T. D. ATKINSON. *et al. Excavations at Phylakopi in Melos* (*JHS Suppl. Paper no. 4*). London. 1904.

2. C. W. BLEGEN. *Korakou*. Concord, New Hampshire. 1921.

3. —. *Zygouries*. Cambridge, Mass. 1928.

4. —. *Prosymna*. Cambridge University Press. 1937.

5. C. W. BLEGEN *et al. Troy*. Vols. III & IV. Princeton. 1953–8.

6. O. FRÖDIN and A. W. PERSSON. *Asine*. Stockholm. 1938

7. E. GJERSTAD *et al. Swedish Cyprus Expedition*. 4 vols. Stockholm. 1927–1935, 1948.

8. H. GOLDMAN. *Eutresis*. Cambridge, Mass. 1931.

9. W. A. HEURTLEY. *Prehistoric Macedonia*. Cambridge. 1939.

10. H. G. LOLLING. *Das Kuppelgrab bei Menidi*. Athens. 1880.

11. A. S. MURRAY *et al. Excavations in Cyprus*. London. 1900.

12. G. E. MYLONAS. Προϊστορικὴ ᾿Ελευσίς. Athens. 1932.

13. A. W. PERSSON. *Royal Tombs at Dendra*. Lund. 1931.

14. —. *New Tombs at Dendra*. Lund. 1942.

15. SIR W. M. F. PETRIE. *Tell el-Amarna*. London. 1894.

16. C. F. A. SCHAEFFER. *Enkomi-Alasia*. Paris. 1952.

17. HEINRICH SCHLIEMANN. *Mycenae*. London. 1878.

18. —. *Orchomenos*. Leipzig. 1881.

19. —. *Tiryns*. Leipzig. 1886.

20. *Tiryns. Die Ergebnisse der Ausgrabungen des Instituts.* Vols. I, II. Athens. 1912. Vol. III. Augsburg. 1930.
21. M. N. VALMIN. *The Swedish Messenia Expedition.* Lund. 1938.
22. A. J. B. WACE. *Chamber Tombs at Mycenae.* Oxford. 1932.
23. C. WALDSTEIN, editor. *The Argive Heraeum.* Vol. II. Cambridge, Mass. 1905.

In addition to the above consult

GEORG KARO. Mykenische Kultur. In *Pauly Wissowa*, Suppl. VI (1935). Contains a very complete bibliography up to 1935.
BRENDA E. MOON. *Mycenaean Civilization, Publications since 1935. Bibliography. Institute of Classical Studies, University of London, Bulletin Supplement.* No. 3. 1957.
BRENDA E. MOON. *Mycenaean Civilization, Publications 1956–60. A second bibliography. Institute of Classical Studies, University of London, Bulletin Supplement* No. 12. 1961.

And for the latest and current publications consult the bibliographies in
EMMETT L. BENNETT, editor. *Nestor. Institute for research in the Humanities.* University of Wisconsin.

INTRODUCTION.

C. W. BLEGEN. *The Mycenaean Age.* Cincinnati. 1962. Includes an up-to-date account of excavations in Greece.
JOHN CHADWICK. *The Decipherment of Linear B.* Cambridge. 1958. Chapter 2.
N. G. L. HAMMOND. *A History of Greece.* Oxford. 1959. Chapters 1 and 2.
DENYS L. PAGE. *History and the Homeric Iliad.* Berkeley, California. 1959. Chapter II.
A. J. B. WACE. The Arrival of the Greeks. In *Viking.* 1954. (*Norsk Arkeologisk Selskap.* Oslo.)

For the excavations by the different foreign Schools consult the bibliography in.

A. FURUMARK. *The Mycenaean Pottery.* Stockholm. 1941, p. 644, where the pottery found in these excavations is listed alphabetically under sites.

CHAPTER I. WRITTEN SOURCES:
LINEAR B AND TRADITION.

Linear B.

Emmett L. Bennett. *The Mycenae Tablets.* Philadelphia. 1953.
—. *The Mycenae Tablets II.* Philadelphia. 1958.
—. *The Pylos Tablets.* Princeton. 1955.
John Chadwick. *The Decipherment of Linear B.* Cambridge. 1958.
—. *The Mycenae Tablets III.* Philadelphia. 1963.
Sir Arthur Evans. *Scripta Minoa I.* Oxford. 1909.
A.E.Kober. *Inflection in Linear Class B. AJA* 50, 1946.
J. L. Myres, *editor. Scripta Minoa II.* Oxford. 1952.
L.R.Palmer. *Achaeans and Indo Europeans.* Oxford. 1955
M.G.F.Ventris and John Chadwick. *Documents in Mycenaean Greek.*
    Cambridge. 1956.

Tradition.

T.W.Allen. *The Homeric Catalogue of Ships.* Oxford. 1921.
Sir Maurice Bowra. *Heroic Poetry.* London. 1952.
—, *Homer and his forerunners.* Edinburgh. 1955.
—. *Tradition and design in the Iliad.* Oxford. 1930. (repr. 1958)
M.I.Finley. *The world of Odysseus.* London. 1956.
G.S.Kirk. *The Songs of Homer.* Cambridge. 1962.
H.L.Lorimer. *Homer and the Monuments.* London. 1950.

CHAPTER II. THE POTTERY AND CHRONOLOGY.

Per Ålin. *Das Ende der mykenischen Fundstätten auf dem griechischen Fest-
    land.* Lund. 1962.
C.W.Blegen. Troy. *CAH,* Fascicle 1. Cambridge. 1961.
Corpus Vasorum Antiquorum. Paris. 1922–
N. de G.Davies. *The Tomb of Rekh-mi-re at Thebes,* 2 vols. New York.
    1943.
V.R.d'A.Desborough and N.G.L.Hammond. The end of Mycen-
    aean civilization and the Dark Age. *CAH,* Fascicle 13, 1962.

Sir John Forsdyke. *Greece before Homer*. London. 1956.

Elizabeth French. Pottery groups from Mycenae: a summary. *BSA*, 1963, 44.

A. Furtwängler and G. Loeschcke. *Mykenische Vasen*. Berlin. 1886.

A. Furumark. *The Chronology of Mycenaean Pottery*. Stockholm. 1941.

—. *The Mycenaean Pottery*. Stockholm. 1941.

V. Hankey. Late Helladic tombs at Khalkis. *BSA*, 1952, 49.

W.C.Hayes *et al.* Chronology: Egypt, Western Asia and the Aegean Bronze Age. *CAH*. Fascicle 4. 1962.

J.D.S.Pendlebury. *Tell el-Amarna*. London. 1935.

—. Egypt and the Aegean in the Late Bronze Age. *Journal of Egyptian Archaeology*, 1930, 75.

Sir W.M.F.Petrie. *Kahun, Gurob and Hawara*. London. 1890.

F.H.Stubbings. The Mycenaean pottery of Attica. *BSA*, 1947, 1.

—. Some Mycenaean artists. *BSA*, 1951, 168.

A.J.B.Wace. Ephyraean Ware. *BSA*, 1956, 123.

—. The chronology of Late Helladic III B. *BSA*, 1957, 220.

A.J.B.Wace and C.W.Blegen. Pottery as evidence for Trade and Colonisation. *Klio*, 1939, 131.

For illustrations of pottery see also 1 – 23 under *General*.

CHAPTER III. RELIGION AND BURIAL CUSTOMS.

Archaeological Reports for 1958. p. 4. for Marathon horse burial.

C.W.Blegen. Excavations at Pylos 1953. *AJA*, 1954, 27. Contains a section on the large tholos tomb.

C.W.Blegen and Mabel Lang. Palace of Nestor excavations of 1957. *AJA*, 1958, 175. Sections on the small tholos and on the unplundered chamber tomb.

J.L.Caskey. Royal Shaft Graves at Lerna. *Archaeology*, 1960, 130

—. Excavations in Keos, 1960–61, *Hesperia*, 1962, 263. Account of the discovery of the life-sized terracottahead.

H. Gallet de Santerre. *Délos primitive et archaïque*. Paris. 1958.

W.K.C.Guthrie. *The Greeks and their Gods*. London. 1950.

—. The Religion and Mythology of the Greeks. *CAH*. Fascicle 2. Cambridge. 1961.

M.S.F.Hood. Tholos tombs of the Aegean. *Antiquity*, 1960, 166.

GEORG KARO. *Die Schachtgräber von Mykenai*. Munich. 1930.

S.N.MARINATOS. Excavations near Pylos, 1956. *Antiquity*, 1957, 97.

G.E.MYLONAS. *Ancient Mycenae*. London. 1957. Particularly for an account of Grave Circle B.

G. E. MYLONAS, *editor*. In *Studies presented to David M. Robinson*. I. St. Louis. 1951–3. The Cult of the Dead in Helladic times.

M.P.NILSSON. *The Minoan-Mycenaean Religion*. 2nd ed. Lund. 1950.

A.W.PERSSON. *The religion of Greece in prehistoric times*. Los Angeles. 1942.

C. PICARD. *Les religions préhelléniques*. Paris. 1948.

See also 2–4, 6, 7, 10–14, 21–23, under *General*.

CHAPTER IV. THE HOUSES OF THE LIVING AND THE DEAD.

EMMETT L.BENNETT, *editor*. *The Mycenae Tablets II*. Philadelphia. 1958. The Introduction deals with the Houses outside the Citadel.

C.W.BLEGEN. The palace of Nestor; excavations at Pylos 1952–56. *AJA* 57–61.

—. An early tholos tomb in Western Messenia. *Hesperia*, 1954, 158.

C.W.BLEGEN and MABEL LANG. The Palace of Nestor excavations 1957–62. *AJA* 62–7.

OSCAR BRONEER. Athens in the Late Bronze Age. *Antiquity*, 1956, 9.

JOHN CHADWICK, *editor*. *The Mycenae Tablets III*. Philadelphia. 1963. Sections on the West House, House of Sphinxes, and Citadel House.

E.J.A.KENNEY. The ancient drainage of the Copais. *Liverpool Annals of Arch. and Anth.*, 1935, 182.

K. MÜLLER. *Tiryns. Die Ergebnisse der Ausgrabungen*. Vol. 3. Augsburg. 1930.

G.E.MYLONAS. *Ancient Mycenae*. London. 1957.

G.A.PAPAVASILEIOU. Περὶ τῶν ἐν Εὐβοίᾳ ἀρχαίων τάφων. Athens. 1910.

D.A.THEOCHARES. Iolkos, whence sailed the Argonauts. *Archaeology*, 1958, 13.

J. THREPSIADES. Reports on excavations at Gla. In *Ergon* 1955–60.

A.J.B.WACE *et al*. Excavations at Mycenae. *BSA* 25 (1921–3).

—. Mycenae 1939–54. Part 4. *BSA*, 1955, 175.

For house plans see also 2, 3, 6, 8, 21 under *General*.

For fortress plans see 1, 6, 14, 17, 20.
For tholoi see 10, 13, 21.

CHAPTER V. DAILY LIFE AND THE ARTS.

GEORGE F. BASS. A Bronze Age shipwreck. *Expedition,* 1961, 2.

EMMETT L. BENNETT, *editor. The Mycenae Tablets II.* Philadelphia. 1958. The Introduction gives an account of important finds in the Houses outside the Citadel.

ELIZABETH PIERCE BLEGEN in *Prosymna.* Cambridge. 1937. Chapter VII, Jewellery and ornaments.

JOHN CHADWICK. *The Decipherment of Linear B.* Cambridge. 1958. Chapter 7.

HELENE J. KANTOR. *The Aegean and the Orient in the second millennium B.C.* Bloomington, Indiana. 1947.

GEORG KARO. *Die Schachtgräber von Mykenai.* Munich. 1930.

H. L. LORIMER. *Homer and the Monuments.* London. 1950. Chapter VI, Dress.

G. LOUD. *The Megiddo ivories.* Chicago. 1939.

S. N. MARINATOS. Excavations near Pylos, 1956. *Antiquity,* 1957, 97.

G. RODENWALDT. *Tiryns.* Vol. II. Athens. 1912.

—. *Der Fries des Megarons von Mykenai.* Halle. 1921.

C. TSOUNTAS. Concerning the tomb at Vapheio. *Ephemeris* 1889, 129.

See also 4, 13, 14, 22, under *General.*

CHAPTER VI. WAR AND TRADE.

JOHN CHADWICK. *The Decipherment of Linear B.* Cambridge. 1958. Chapter 7.   WAR

M. S. F. HOOD. *Archaeological Reports* 1960–61, p. 9 on the bronze coat of mail from Dendra.

GEORG KARO. *Die Schachtgräber von Mykenai.* Munich 1930.

H. L. LORIMER. *Homer and the Monuments.* London. 1950. Chapter V, Arms and Armour.

G. RODENWALDT. *Tiryns.* Vol. II. Athens. 1912.

N. K. SANDARS. The first Aegean swords and their ancestry. *AJA,* 1961, 17.

TRADE

GEORGE F. BASS A Bronze Age shipwreck. *Expedition*, 1961, 2.

L. BERNABÒ BREA. *Sicily before the Greeks*. London. 1957.

V. G. CHILDE. *The Dawn of European Civilization*. London. 1957.

O. G. S. CRAWFORD. The symbols carved on Stonehenge. *Antiquity*, 1954, 25.

J. GARSTANG. *Prehistoric Mersin*. Oxford. 1953.

H. GOLDMAN. *Excavations at Gözlü Kule, Tarsus*. Princeton. 1956.

J. D. S. PENDLEBURY. *Aegyptiaca*. Cambridge. 1930.

SIR W. M. F. PETRIE. *Tell el Amarna*. London. 1894.

J. F. S. STONE. *Wessex before the Celts*. London. 1958.

F. H. STUBBINGS. *Mycenaean pottery from the Levant*. Cambridge. 1951.

—. A winged axe mould. *BSA*, 1954, 297.

D. A. THEOCHARES. Iolkos, whence sailed the Argonauts. *Archaeology*, 1958, 13.

LORD WILLIAM TAYLOUR. *Mycenean pottery in Italy*. Cambridge. 1958.

A. J. B. WACE and C. W. BLEGEN. Pottery as evidence for trade and colonisation in the Aegean Bronze Age. *Klio*, 1939, 131.

CARL WEICKERT. Die Ausgrabung beim Athena Tempel im Milet. In *Istanbuler Mitt.* 7 (1957), and 9, 10 (1959–1960).

See also 1, 8, 9, 13, 22, under *General*.

CHAPTER VII. THE RISE AND FALL OF MYCENAE.

PER ÅLIN. *Das Ende der mykenischen Fundstätten auf dem griechischen Festland*. Lund 1962.

J. BÉRARD. *La colonisation grecque*. Paris. 1957.

C. W. BLEGEN. Troy. *CAH* Fascicle 1. Cambridge. 1961.

—. *Troy and the Trojans*. London. 1963.

OSCAR BRONEER. Athens in the Late Bronze Age. *Antiquity*, 1956, 9.

—. The Corinthian isthmus and the Isthmian Sanctuary. *Antiquity*, 1958, 80.

V. R. d'A. DESBOROUGH and N. G. L. HAMMOND. The end of the Mycenaean civilization and the Dark Age. *CAH* Fascicle 13. 1962.

SIR ALAN GARDINER. *Egypt of the Pharaohs*. Oxford. 1961.

O. R. GURNEY. *The Hittites*. Harmondsworth. 1954.

G. L. HUXLEY. *Achaeans and Hittites*. Oxford. 1960.

A. D. KERAMOPOULLOS. The House of Kadmos. *Ephemeris*, 1909, 57.

—. Excavations at Thebes. *Deltion* 3, 1917.

DENYS L. PAGE. *History and the Homeric Iliad.* Berkeley, California. 1959. Chapters I–III.

J. D. S. PENDLEBURY. *The archaeology of Crete.* London. 1939. Chapter V.

F. H. STUBBINGS. The rise of Mycenaean Civilization. *CAH* Fascicle 18. 1963.

See also 1 under *General.*

Sources of Illustrations

I should like to thank the many individuals and institutions who have been of such great assistance in my work and in particular those who have made available photos and/or drawings for use in this book.

The sources of the plates used are as follows: Professor C. W. Blegen, 14, 36, 37, 38, 39; Professor J. L. Caskey, 19; Professor Max Hirmer, 3, 4, 7, 8, 10, 11, 12, 15, 16, 17, 18, 20, 21, 22, 23, 27, 28, 31, 32, 43, 44, 46, 47, 48, 49, 50, 51, 52, 53, 55, 57, 58, 59, 61, 63, 66; Professor Jessen, Deutsches Archäologisches Institut, 9; Robert McCabe, 35; E. Stikas of the Greek Archaeological Service, 29; Dr. F. H. Stubbings and Messrs. MacMillan & Co., 54, 62, 64; Thames & Hudson archives, 1, 5, 42, 56; Dr N. Verdelis, 40, 65; Mrs Alan Wace, 2, 13, 41, 45, 60. [Numbers 6, 24, 25, 26, 30, 33 and 34 are by the author.] The drawings in plates 38, 54 and 60 were the work of Piet de Jong.

The maps, figures 1 and 63, were drawn by Mr H. A. Shelley of Cambridge, figure 67 by Michael Spink of Thames & Hudson, and figure 28 reproduced by courtesy of the British School of Archaeology at Athens from the drawing of Piet de Jong. Dr F. H. Stubbings and Messrs. Macmillan & Co., kindly gave their permission for the use of figures 2, 3, 8, 9, 10, 12, 14, 17, 21, 22, 25, 30, 31, 33, 35, 37, 43 and 51 from *A Companion to Homer* by Wace and Stubbings. Mr Michael Langham Rowe of Cambridge drew the bulk of the figures used, numbers, 4, 5, 6, 7, 11, 13, 15, 16, 18, 19, 20, 23, 24, 36, 38, 39, 40, 42, 44, 45, 46, 47, 48, 49, 50, 53, 54, 55, 56, 57, 58, 59, 60, 61, 62, 64, 65, 66, 68, 70, 71, 72, 73 and 74.

1

2

3

4

8

9

10

11

12   13

14

16

19

20

21

22

25

24

26

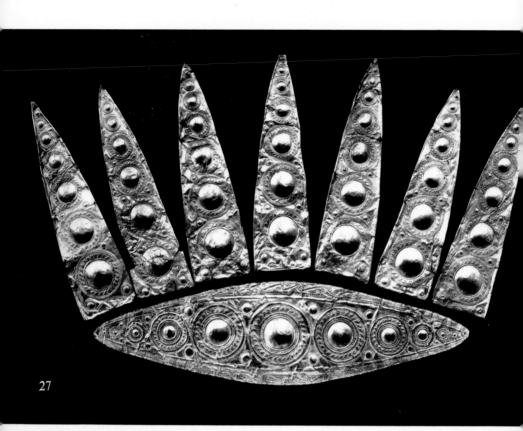

27

28

30

31

32

33

34

35

38

39

41

40

42

43

44

45

46

47

48

49

50

51

52

54

55

56

57

58

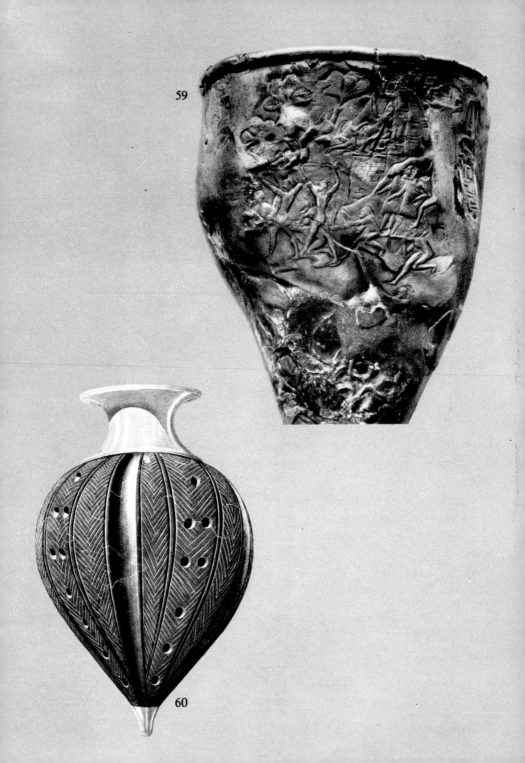

59

60

61

62

63

64

65

66

1   Stirrup-jar, pilgrim flask, alabastron, and spouted jug. LH IIIA. The first and third of the illustrated vases are frequently found in excavations. The stirrup-jar (so-called from the handles holding the false spout which suggest a stirrup) was perhaps used for oil or unguents. The pilgrim flask was very popular in the Near East. The spouted jug is sometimes referred to as a feeding-bottle.

2   Tablet Ge 606 from the House of Sphinxes, Mycenae. $3\frac{3}{4}$ in. by $2\frac{1}{2}$ in. Mid-thirteenth century B.C. Most of the tablets found in this house deal with herbs, spices, and condiments. This particular tablet lists quanti-ties of coriander, cumin, white safflower, fennel seed, sesame, red [saf-flower] and mint.

3, 4   Two gold cups from a tholos tomb at Vapheio. Upper diameter $4\frac{1}{4}$ in. The tholos, now much ruined, is near the village of Vapheio and about 3 miles south of Sparta. These magnificent cups escaped the attention of the tomb robbers. Vivid scenes connected with bull-hunting and the capture of the bull are portrayed in repoussé work on the two cups. The detail of the cup (Plate 4) shows the tethering of the bull after it has been taken unawares while courting a decoy cow (visible on the right). The section of the second cup (Plate 3) shows the bull charging two athletes with dire effect. Late fifteenth century B.C.

5   Kylix. Zygouries style. LH IIIB. A great quantity of kylikes in this style was found in the 'Potter's shop' at Zygouries. They are probably all by the same artist. The elements in the design have been selected from several well-known Mycenaean motives such as the octopus, palm, flow-er, and tongue pattern, and combined into a new unitary and highly stylised creation.

6   Palace Style jar from Messenia. Height $c.$ $30\frac{1}{2}$ in. These jars were very fashionable in the Palace of Knossos during the late fifteenth century

B.C. but the greater number of them are found on the Greek mainland. This jar, from a tholos tomb in Messenia, contained a burial. Other types of vases decorated in this florid manner are usually described as being in the Palace Style.

7 Krater. The Warrior Vase. LH III C. Height $16\frac{1}{2}$ in. This deep bowl was found by Schliemann in a house excavated by him immediately to the south of Grave Circle A (see Fig. 35 F, p. 99). It shows soldiers marching off to battle, while a disconsolate woman (on the left) waves them farewell. The scene provides one of our sources of information concerning the battle-dress and armour of the period. Twelfth century B.C.

8 Gold signet ring from Mycenae. Maximum diameter 1.3 in. From a treasure found to the south of Grave Circle A. A religious scene, variously interpreted; some see in it a representation of the Mycenaean pantheon (sun, moon, goddesses, and a god armed with the figure-of-eight shield and spear). The principal figure is the goddess sitting under the sacred tree and holding three poppies. The other women holding lilies in their hands are perhaps votaries. The god may be the Divine Son. In the centre of the picture is a double axe.

9 Painted limestone tablet, Mycenae. Length $7\frac{1}{2}$ in. Found in a house excavated by Professor Tsountas (see Fig. 35 H, p. 99) and datable to LH III. The central figure is a goddess armed with a figure-of-eight shield. On either side of her is a votary with hands raised in adoration. To the right of the goddess in an altar.

10 Gold signet ring from Mycenae. Maximum diameter $1\frac{1}{8}$ in. The tree cult seems to figure prominently in this frenzied scene on a ring from a chamber tomb at Mycenae. The tree, over a shrine enclosing a pillar, is being frantically shaken by a youth, perhaps to attract the attention of the Tree Goddess. In the centre is a dancing woman. The woman on the right laments over a shrine enclosing another pillar. This has been interpreted as a tomb, and some recognise in this scene the lamentations over the death of the vegetation god.

11 Faïence statuette of a goddess with snakes. Knossos. Height $11\frac{3}{4}$ in. From the storeroom of the sanctuary. This is the smaller of the two

statuettes in faïence found in the storeroom. The Mother Goddess is here represented in her aspect as guardian of the home, the Snake goddess. Her dress shows the fashion of the period (early sixteenth century).

2, 13 Ivory group from Mycenae. Height 2½ in. Found at the foot of the Archaic temple which was probably built on the site of the Mycenaean sanctuary. The group could represent the divine triad of Eleusis, but others prefer a secular interpretation. Exquisite workmanship of the LH III period.

14 Palace of Nestor, Pylos. The great hearth. Diameter *c.* 13 ft. The hearth was the central feature of the throne-room. The surround, or border, is covered in stucco and painted with a pattern of running spirals in three or more colours on its upper surface. The vertical edge of the surround is decorated with tongues of flame. Breaks in the stucco reveal the identical pattern on earlier plaster work and show that the hearth had been restored many times.

15 The Lion Gate, Mycenae. Two lionesses, now headless, stand guard over the entrance to the Citadel of Mycenae. Between them is a column which supports on an abacus a row of four roundels. These represent the ends of un-squared timbers used as joists for an upper floor. This combination could therefore represent a building, the palace itself, the lionesses of Mycenae being its guardians. But this same combination also stands for a shrine and it should be noted that the forequarters of of beasts stand on two altars (*cf.* Plate 9), so that a religious interpretation is also permissible. Some consider the whole composition to be purely heraldic. Beyond the gate, constructed of four great monoliths – the weight of the lintel alone is estimated at 20 tons, – can be seen the ascending Great Ramp (the steps have been made for the benefit of tourists and do not belong to the original scheme).

16 Gold funeral-mask. The so-called Agamemnon. Grave Circle A. Height 10½ in. Early fifteenth century. When Schliemann uncovered these noble features in Shaft Grave V, he telegraphed the Kaiser that he had 'gazed on the face of Agamemnon'. There were five gold masks found in Grave Circle A and according to Schliemann they were laid over the faces of

the deceased. This recalls Egyptian burial custom where the features of the dead man were reproduced on the anthropomorphic coffin.

17 Gold rhyton in the form of a lion's head from Shaft Grave IV. Height 8 in. LH I. It is apparently hammered out of a single sheet of gold. Rhytons, or fillers, are often funnel-shaped (*cf.* Fig. 24, p. 73) and as such they would normally be used for practical purposes (as we use funnels today, i.e., to avoid spilling the liquid); but animal-shaped rhytons were almost certainly used for cult purposes, particularly when they were made in precious metals as here. Other examples from Shaft Grave IV (the richest of all the graves) include a magnificent bull's head in silver and gold and a silver stag. Animal rhytons were also carved in marble as we know from the fragment of a lioness's head found at Delphi.

18 Funeral mask from Grave Circle B. Height 8¾ in. Sixteenth century B.C. This was the only mask found in this Grave Circle and it was not laid over the face of the deceased but close by. It is not certain whether that was its original position or whether it was moved there on the occasion of a later burial. There are holes by the ears for fastening. The mask is made of electrum which is an alloy of silver and gold.

19 Terracotta head of a goddess. Keos. Height 7¾ in. An important find from recent excavations, showing that cult statues of human size existed in Mycenaean times. Other fragments of cult statues have been uncovered on this same site. They date from the last phase of LH III.

20 Grave Stela from Grave Circle A. Height 4 ft 5 in. Width 3 ft 6 in. Stelae were more common in Grave Circle A than in B. Seventeen stelae were found in A of which six were undecorated. The best preserved examples, of which this is one, were found over Shaft Grave V. The decorative spirals are comparatively well executed, the principal scene less so; the animal drawing the chariot looks more like a bull than a horse. The naked figure (holding a spear?) in front of the horse is generally interpreted as an enemy being ridden down by the warrior in the chariot. The latter is armed with a weapon that may be a type B rapier (Fig. 58, p. 147)

21 Grave Circle A within the walls of the Citadel, Mycenae. A view from
the south-east. The new enclosure wall, or *temenos*, of which the entrance
can be seen on the right, was built in the thirteenth century B.C. (or the
fourteenth according to others). It consists of two parallel rows of upright
slabs that were originally roofed (see the reconstruction in Fig. 28, p. 78).
One cover-slab can be seen in position near the entrance. The six shaft
graves are in the west part of the Circle. Here the depth is so great that
a modern retaining wall is necessary to support the *temenos*. Beyond can
be seen the inner face of the Cyclopean walls which had to be extended
in this area to include the sacred enclosure within the fortifications.

22 The dromos and doorway of the so-called Treasury of Atreus, Mycenae.
This is the name that Pausanias gave to this monumental tomb of the
thirteenth century B.C. (or according to others, late fourteenth century).
The doorway is 18 feet high and 9 feet wide at the base. The depth of
the entrance is 18 feet 4 inches. It is roofed by two monolithic lintels,
of which the inner one is estimated to weigh over 100 tons. Note the
'relieving triangle' above the doorway. Its purpose was to divert the
great weight of the superstructure from the lintels on to the massive door
jambs. The dromos, as in other later tholos tombs at Mycenae, is lined
with enormous ashlar blocks of coglomerate. Its length is 120 feet.

23 The so-called Treasury of Atreus, Mycenae. A view from inside the
tomb, with the entrance from the dromos on the right. The inner of the
two lintels over the entrance, estimated to weigh more than 100 tons, is
partly visible. Facing is a smaller door with lintel and relieving triangle
that leads into a side chamber, 20 feet square, cut in the rock. The diameter of the tholos itself is 49 feet and its height 45 feet.

24 Burials in a ruined tholos tomb near the Palace of Nestor at Pylos. Only
a part of the foundations of the tholos survive. The dromos has not been
preserved. It is estimated that the tomb contained 23 burials dating from
the sixteenth and fifteenth centuries. The last burial was laid out at full
length in the centre of the tomb. The remains of previous obsequies were
pushed aside to make place for it and then stuffed into pits; except for four
burials of an earlier period which had been put into large pithoi or storage
jars. By the side of two of these jars were placed bronze cauldrons, rapiers,
and other weapons.

25 Extended burial in the tholos tomb illustrated in Plate 24. This was the last body to be laid out in the tomb and dates from the end of the fifteenth or very beginning of the fourteenth century. Objects treasured by the deceased in life had been laid on or around his body.

26 Figurine found on the chest of the skeleton illustrated in Plate 25. This is one of the earliest Mycenaean figurines known. (None of the pottery from this tholos was later than LH II/III, or the end of the fifteenth century B.C.) It is much more naturalistic than the later figurines. The arms are not only modelled but are set apart from the body. In later examples the arms are placed close to the body and ultimately merge with it to form the φ type of figurine.

27 Gold diadem. Shaft Grave III, Mycenae. Width 26 in. From a woman's grave. The dimensions of this 'tiara' are enormous and it would have been a problem indeed to wear it in life. An almost identical diadem, but without the 'rays', was found in the little tholos near the Palace of Nestor at Pylos. It was very much smaller and therefore more practicable. It was found broken in three pieces and for that reason no doubt escaped spoliation.

28 Dagger blade from a tholos at Routsi, Messenia. Length of blade 10 in. This superb example of gold, silver, and niello inlay work stands comparison with the famous dagger blades from Grave Circle A at Mycenae. It is dated about 1500 B.C. The scene depicts nautili moving on the ocean bed among stylised rocks and seaweed.

29 Horse burial in the dromos of a tholos near Marathon, Attica. This surprising discovery only came to light fairly recently with the re-excavation of the dromos of this tomb. It throws a new and unexpected light on Mycenaean burial customs, and recalls the 'death-pit' burials of Ur of more than a thousand years earlier.

30 The entrance to a large tholos tomb near the Palace of Nestor, Pylos. This must have been an extremely rich tomb as, although it was thoroughly plundered, many objects of value were overlooked, including the Griffin Seal (Plate 55) and the gold figure-of-eight shield pendant

(Plate 63). Quantities of gold leaf fragments were found in the disturbed soil and large pieces of it were still adhering to the earthen floor of the tomb. The doorway was blocked by a solidly built wall over 6 feet in depth, but its upper courses had been disturbed, presumably by tomb-robbers of earlier times who gained access to the tholos in this way.

31   The tholos illustrated in Plate 30, after excavation. The blocking wall has been removed, one of the broken lintels replaced, and the dome restored. The dromos was cut in the natural, very soft rock (marl). Its sides were originally vertical but they have now collapsed under the effect of winter rains. The diameter of the tomb is about 31 feet. It appears to have been constructed in the latter part of the sixteenth century.

32   Entrance to a chamber tomb at Volymidia, near Chora, Messenia. In the earlier chamber tombs (LH I), such as this one, the dromos is short and wide, and it slopes down steeply towards the tomb. Sometimes a pit for a secondary burial was excavated in the floor of the dromos. In this case it had been cut in the side wall.

33   The blocked doorway of the tomb referred to in Plate 34. In this, the later type of chamber-tomb (LH III B), the dromos is narrow. After each burial the door was blocked with a stone wall which had to be taken down (in part at least) for the next funeral. In front of the wall can be seen a small rough pillar, or 'marker', the significance of which is not clear.

34   Pottery and skeletal remains found in an unplundered chamber tomb near the Palace of Nestor, Pylos. LH III B. The remains belong to an earlier burial which have been pushed unceremoniously aside with the grave goods to make room for the latest occupant. Among the pottery can be seen a stirrup-jar and an alabastron on the left. In the centre is a three-handled jar covered with fragments of a bowl, and on the right is a jug. These are painted in the III B style.

35   The Citadel of Mycenae from the east. This is not the usual view of the famous acropolis, which is normally approached from the south-west. Here, however, it is seen without the background of the Mounts Elias

and Zara which, though impressive, tend to reduce it to insignificance. It is perhaps more appropriately viewed from the Perseia spring on which it relied for its existence.

36 View of the island of Sphakteria from the Palace of Nestor, Pylos, and from the east. At the north end of the island (right centre) is the site of the famous defeat of the Spartans by the Athenians in the Peloponnesian war. The island guards the entrance to the Bay of Navarino, one of the finest harbours in the world.

37 View of the Palace of Nestor, Pylos, from the south-east (*cf.* also Fig. 33, p. 94). In the foreground is the propylon with the archives room on the left. Beyond the court lie the royal apartments: porch, vestibule, and the great hall or megaron. The queen's apartments are on the right.

38 The so-called Orpheus fresco from the throne-room of the Palace of Nestor, Pylos. Restored drawing. The lyre-player is seated on a rock which, like the clouds above him, is portrayed according to the Minoan convention. His dress is unusual and it may be a priestly garb. The large bird which perhaps is being charmed by the music of the lyre has suggested the title of this fresco.

39 The bathroom adjoining the queen's megaron in the Palace of Nestor, Pylos. This room was not directly accessible from the queen's apartments. It was not therefore a private bathroom. It could readily be placed at the disposal of an honoured guest. Much care had been expended on the appurtenances of this room (the bath itself was elaborately painted) as much as to suggest that a bath was something of a ritual. An habitual bath is a modern conception.

40 Mycenae. Houses outside the Citadel, viewed from the acropolis. The three houses excavated by Professor Wace are alongside the old road to the acropolis. From left to right they are: House of Sphinxes, House of the Oil Merchant, House of Shields (*cf.* Fig. 36, p. 101). Beyond is the new road, then in course of construction. While this work was being carried out a new house, the West House, was uncovered. This has been excavated by N. Verdelis, Ephor for the Argolid.

41 The Grand Staircase, Mycenae. The first flight is completely preserved. The man is standing on the first landing, from which the second flight, presumably constructed of wood, would ascend in the reverse direction and parallel to the lower flight. The second landing led directly into the palace (the south entrance) which was supported on this side by the terrace wall visible on the left. (see also Fig. 50, p. 133)

42 Entrance passage leading to the Perseia cistern and built within the Cyclopean fortress walls. Access to the secret cistern was by means of three flights of steps. The first flight (seen here) passed through the 18 foot-thick fortress wall and through a doorway of monoliths to a landing, from which the two lower underground flights descended in two sharp bends to the reservoir (*cf.* Fig. 40, p. 107). The roof of the passage was constructed on the corbel principle, which is clearly demonstrated in this photograph.

43 The North Gate of the fortress of Gla. The plain beyond is the former Lake Copais. Little is known about this, the largest of all the Mycenaean fortresses. Although much denuded, the ruins of the 3,000 yard-long encircling walls, Cyclopean-built, stand out very clearly. The North Gate is comparatively well preserved. The latest pottery found on the site was LH IIIB.

44 The west bastion (in the foreground) guarding the entrance to the Lion Gate, Mycenae. Comparatively little reconstruction work has been carried out on this side of the acropolis and the photograph provides a good example of the grandeur of Cyclopean masonry. The main entrance to the Citadel, the Lion Gate, is concealed by the west bastion, from which a murderous onslaught could be launched against the unshielded (right) side of the enemy making a frontal attack on the gate, since the shield would be carried on the left arm.

45 Ivory plaque of confronted sphinxes, from the House of Sphinxes. Width 3 in. LH IIIB. This justly famed ivory carving has given its name to the house in which it was found. The sphinx is an oriental creation and so is the antithetical composition, but the other elements, the horns of consecration and the fluted column with a 'Pergamene' capital, are Mycenaean.

46 Citadel of Tiryns. The South Gallery. There are two such galleries constructed within the Cyclopean walls, the second being on the east side of the fortress. The gallery has access to storage rooms on the left. These also had embrasures from which the enemy could be harassed by fire. Note the corbelled roofing.

47 Fresco fragment from the palace at Tiryns. Restored drawing. This is part of the great fresco of a procession of women. Only very small fragments have survived, but they are sufficient to give a good idea of the costume worn at the time (LH III). It was very similar to that portrayed in Minoan art.

48 Gold jewellery from Prosymna in the Argolid. Diameter of rosette $\frac{7}{8}$ in. LH III. The subsidiary beads to the rosettes take the form of stylised papyrus plants.

49 Gold jewellery from Prosymna in the Argolid. The subsidiary beads to the rosette are here lilies. This type of rosette was also worn as an earring.

50 Gold earrings from Shaft Grave III. Diameter 3 in. These massive earrings were each made of two plates, secured together by gold wire. They were suspended on spiral rings which pierced the ears.

51 Gold funeral-pectoral from Shaft Grave V. Height $14\frac{1}{2}$ in. This was laid over the body that wore the gold-mask illustrated in Plate 16, wrongly identified by Schliemann as that of Agamemnon. A second gold pectoral, but plain, was found with another skeleton in this grave.

52 Silver cup with inlaid male heads. From a chamber tomb at Mycenae. Diameter $6\frac{1}{2}$ in. LH III. Gold and niello inlay-work. Similar gold heads, probably from a cup of this type, were found in the palace at Pylos. The heads show the hair-style of the period and that the upper lip was often shaven. The band of decoration on the cup is a motive frequently used on vases of LH II.

53 Lead figure of a youth. From a tholos tomb at Kampos, Laconia.

Height 4¾ in. The style of this figure is Minoan, notably the slender waist and the loin-cloth with cod-piece. Figures in the round, except for clay figurines, are comparatively rare in Mycenaean art and in this material (lead) unique.

54 Fresco with warriors and horses, from Mycenae. Restored drawing. Only fragments of this fresco are preserved and they do not provide complete evidence for the everyday dress of the men. The short-sleeved tunic is illustrated but the short 'skirt' and leggings are substantiated by other sources (*cf.* Fig. 39, p. 106). The treatment of the horses' manes calls for comment as it is a characteristic that is not only reproduced in the tablets (see Fig. 53, p. 141) but also in ivory inlays.

55 Gold seal found in the tholos illustrated in Plates 30 and 31. Width 1⅛ in. It was found at the bottom of a grave pit and had escaped the notice of the plunderers. The seal is not of solid gold but has a core of some malleable substance, perhaps bitumen; the back has a finely wrought lattice pattern in gold with paste inlay. Most of the inlay has perished or been lost. In section the seal is elliptical with pointed extremities. It is transversely pierced for suspension. Undoubtedly a royal seal, it belongs stylistically to the latter half of the fifteenth century. The platform on which the royal griffin is couched is decorated with a familiar architectural design, the triglyph and half-rosette motive (see p. 129).

56 The 'Lion Hunt' dagger from Shaft Grave IV. Length 9½ in. A superb example of gold, silver, and niello inlay technique in bronze; of the fifteenth century. Each side of the blade is decorated and in this scene the men are using both figure-of-eight and 'tower' shields. The latter is presumably the type of shield carried by Ajax in the *Iliad*.

57 Gold cup, Vapheio shape, from Shaft Grave IV. Height without handle 2½ in. Many cups of this form, both in gold and silver, were found in the shaft graves, but the manner of their decoration varies greatly. In the present instance a style of horizontal flutings was adopted. A similar technique was used on a gold cup found at Rillaton in Cornwall. The shape of the Rillaton cup is different but it is generally believed that it is actual Mycenaean work or an imitation of it.

58   Gold cup from a tholos at Midea in the Argolid. Diameter 7 in. LH III A. Part of the rich equipment of the King's grave that was fortunately overlooked by the plunderers of the tomb. It is an elegant cup decorated in repoussé and incised technique with marine motives of which the principal recurrent theme is the octopus (on the under-side of the vessel). In the centre are two dolphins; on the left, a row of nautili.

59   Silver funnel-shaped rhyton from Shaft Grave IV. The so-called Siege Rhyton. Existing height 9⅛ in. Upper diameter 4½ in. Much of the vessel has perished and the remaining fragments have been badly put together; the sides should be straight (*cf.* Fig. 24, p. 73). The portion of the rhyton here illustrated shows an enemy city under siege by Mycenaeans. The enemy is attempting to repulse an attack from the sea with arrows and sling stones. The scene on the back of the rhyton is not preserved, but the attitude of the defenders show that the attack is coming from the left and at the base of the vessel (not shown in this photograph) some of the Mycenaeans are shown struggling in the water, their boat having capsized. Only one Mycenaean is illustrated here. He is the figure in the plumed helmet below the defenders. He holds a pole in his right hand and seems to be piloting a boat.

60   Steatite rhyton from the House of Shields. Height 7½ in. LH III B. There were many variations on the simple, but practical, funnel-shaped rhyton. This elegant form in stone (the prototype is Minoan) was originally embellished with inlay, such as coloured stone, paste or other substance.

61   Ivory pyxis (box) from a tholos tomb at Routsi, Messenia. Height *c.* 6 in. This is an example of the earlier style of ivory carving, which is still under Minoan influence. The motives are the running spiral and the sacral ivy leaf. It is dated to about 1500 B.C.

62   Ivory relief of a man wearing a boars'-tusk helmet, from Mycenae. Height 2⅞ in. LH III. There are many such representations in ivory and it is usually thought that they were used as inlays for caskets, etc. From the description in the *Iliad* it is clear that this was the type of helmet that was lent to Odysseus by Meriones. Actual specimens of worked boars' tusks

have been found in several chamber tombs and in one case it was possible to reconstruct an almost complete helmet from them.

63 Miniature figure-of-eight shield of gold from the tholos illustrated in Plates 30 and 31. Height $1\frac{5}{8}$ in. This was found at the bottom of the same pit as the Griffin Seal (Plate 55) and on the same day. It is made of two pieces of gold plate soldered together, of which the upper one is convex, the lower one concave. The shield has two holes at the 'waist' line for suspension. The decoration of the surface with clusters of tiny gold beads shows a high standard of craftsmanship. The ornament is probably to be dated to LH II.

64 Ivory plaque of warrior, from Delos. Height 5 in. Used for the adorn-ment of some piece of furniture, this very effective composition illustrates the main equipment of a Mycenaean soldier: the spear, the figure-of-eight shield, and the boars'-tusk helmet. A certain incongruity exists between the slender Minoan waist and the muscle-bound physique of the warrior.

65 Bronze coat-of-mail (right) found in a chamber tomb at Dendra (Midea); in the centre is a shallow bronze bowl and, on the left, an early style alabastron. This very important and comparatively recent find bears a close resemblance to the type of cuirass which figures on the Knossos tablets, but differs from the cuirass shown on the Pylos tablets (*cf.* Figs. 53, 54, pp. 141, 142). The pottery associated with this find belongs to the transition period LH II/III, or *c.* 1400 B.C. What is now thought to be part of a similar coat-of-mail, the shoulder piece, was found some 25 years earlier in another tomb at Dendra. It was then interpreted as an unusual type of helmet (Fig. 55 b, p. 144).

66 Gold kantharos from Shaft Grave IV. Height $3\frac{5}{8}$ in. An example of the rich variety of forms that were found in this shaft grave. The 'kan-tharos' proper is a Classical two-handled cup, which this find resembles. A gold vessel that seems to copy the form, but does not quite succeed in reproducing its elegance, was found at Fritzdorf in Germany and is probably an imitation.

Index

Numbers in italic type in brackets after place names refer to the Map Figure on which they can be found. Mycenae and Pylos, except for map references, have been excluded from the index as they occur so frequently in the text, references may be found under individual headings, e.g. palaces, etc.

Index

Wace, A.J.B., 17, 117, 229
wanax, 44, 135
weapons, *see* armaments
Wessex, (*63*), 152
West House, 102, 229

wine, 92, 96, 126
wool, 136, 164

Zeus, 61, 62, 63, 64, 67
Zygouries, (*51*), 53, 173, 221